MW01710418

IMAGES
of America

BEVERLY

"VIEWS OF BEVERLY" (C. 1910 POSTCARD). Thirteen of the 14 images on this souvenir postcard appear in this pictorial history of the "Garden City." (Courtesy Kenneth H. Clayton.)

IMAGES
of America

BEVERLY

John Hardy Wright

ARCADIA

ISBN 0-7524-0814-3

First printed in 2000.

Published by Arcadia Publishing,
an imprint of Tempus Publishing, Inc.
2 Cumberland Street
Charleston, SC 29401

Printed in Great Britain.

Library of Congress Catalog Card Number: 00-104031

For all general information contact Arcadia Publishing at:
Telephone 843-853-2070
Fax 843-853-0044
E-Mail sales@arcadiapublishing.com

For customer service and orders:
Toll-Free 1-888-313-2665

Visit us on the internet at http://www.arcadiapublishing.com

This book is dedicated to the memory of Eleanor Broadhead (1909–1999) of Salem, who was a proud descendant of the first Balch in America and an honorary aunt of the author.

Contents

A SOUTHWEST VIEW OF BEVERLY (1839 WOOD ENGRAVING). A gentleman on the Salem shore welcomes the reader to cross the Essex Bridge. The 1,484-foot-long by 34-foot-wide bridge, built on 93 oak supports, was paid for by local shareholders and completed in 1788 at a cost of $16,000. Tolls were collected for 70 years, and the public was free to use it thereafter. In 1789, while on a tour of New England, George Washington dismounted from his steed to examine the bridge's "draw." Goat Hill is not visible at the left end of the bridge, but "Fish Flake Hill" is at the right behind the vessels anchored in the harbor.

INTRODUCTION

"Nature has beautifully delineated Beverly, and marked it for a town."
—Edwin M. Stone, *History of Beverly*, 1843

Nicknamed the Garden City, Beverly, Massachusetts, is located along the shore of Essex County. It was founded in 1626 by a handful of "Old Planters" whose non-garden variety surnames have been perpetuated by local streets and institutions. Referred to as "the Bass River Side" by these first Englishmen, Beverly is bounded on the north by Wenham, on the east by Manchester-by-the-Sea, on the south by the harbor that separates it from Salem, and on the west by Danvers.

Fishing, agriculture, and coastal trade sustained the early inhabitants of the town, which was either named for Beverley, a market town in Yorkshire, England, or "Beaver Lea" for the Beaver Pond located to the right of the larger Norwood's Pond. Roger Conant, one of the town's founders, proposed the name Budleigh to honor his hometown, hoping in turn that it would curtail nonresidents from using the derogatory name "Beggarly." However, the court records of 1671 reveal that this petition did not pass. Active trading with distant countries and the West Indies, not begging, soon brought prosperity and much needed commodities to enterprising merchants of the 18th century up to the Revolutionary War.

Long before Beverly was incorporated as a city in 1894, Cabot Street became the town's main commercial thoroughfare. Businesses of all sorts were established to cater to the needs of the citizenry, and it still serves that purpose today, as does the somewhat parallel Rantoul Street.

The largest 20th-century business venture in Beverly, the United Shoe Machinery Corporation (USM), has been revitalized at the same Elliott Street location today with the renovation of "the Shoe" buildings (the largest reinforced concrete structures in the world before 1905) into the Cummings Center. The USM survived during the Great Depression by cutting back on the workload and keeping most of its large dedicated workforce employed.

Individuals who led simple, day-to-day lives in the city proper coexisted, but not socially, with the landed gentry who acquired breathtaking property along the "Gold Coast" in Pride's Crossing and Beverly Farms beginning around the mid-19th century. The Ayer, Frick, Loring, Swift, and other notable families built magnificent showplaces where they entertained family, friends, and dignitaries without regard to expense. One outstanding and newsworthy person was Eleonora "Eleo" Sears, who excelled in many male-dominated sports and who shocked Californians in 1909 by wearing men's trousers.

The most distinguished personage to enjoy Beverly's salubrious shoreline for a few summers was Pres. William Howard Taft (1909–1913), who maintained an office on Cabot Street, but who much preferred to tour Essex County by automobile as often as he could.

Some early houses and buildings on Fish Flake Hill (a modern name for the historic area between Front and Water Streets) suffered random demolition in 1970. A year later, however, others were saved by dedicated citizens, and the area became designated as the Fish Flake Historic District. With the sympathetic restoration of dwellings there and in other areas of Beverly as well as the stellar renovation of the USM site, the city is well on its way back to economic and aesthetic renewal.

Author's Note: The images in chapter 2 are arranged alphabetically, while those in other chapters appear somewhat geographically. Uncredited images are in the author's collection.

THE *HANNAH* (MID-20TH-CENTURY ILLUSTRATION BY AN UNIDENTIFIED ARTIST). Seamen from another converted fishing-to-schooner-warship admire the first American warship, the two-masted *Hannah,* which was commissioned on September 2, 1775, by Gen. George Washington. (Courtesy Benjamin R. Chadwick.)

One

Patriots, Privateers, and an Early Merchant

EMBRYO OF THE AMERICAN NAVY (MID-19TH-CENTURY ENGRAVING). Two British warships flank the sail-shot schooner *Hannah*, running the gauntlet off Cape Ann on September 5, 1775. Friendly rivalry has existed for many decades between Beverlyites and Marbleheaders over which community's claim of being "the Birthplace of the American Navy" is historically accurate. Named for Col. John Glover's wife, Hannah Gale Glover, the Marblehead fishing schooner was converted to a warship at Glover's Wharf in Beverly, the place from which it sailed with Capt. Nicholson Broughton and his crew. Although *Hannah*'s naval career was "brief, unsuccessful, and troublesome," it was rebuilt and renamed *Lynch* the following year. Its claim to fame is that it was the first of eight vessels (six of which were outfitted and sailed from Beverly Harbor) in the fledgling Continental Navy. (Courtesy Mrs. Samuel E. Swasey.)

BEVERLY MINUTEMEN ON THE MARCH (LATE-18TH-CENTURY WOODCUT). Answering the anticipated alarm at midday on April 19, 1775, were several local patriots whose purpose was to engage the retreating Redcoats. Wounded in the skirmish along Menotomy Road (now Arlington) were Nathaniel Cleaves, William Dodge III, and Samuel Woodbury. Reuben Keniston was killed during the colonists' cause. (Private collection.)

THE GRAVE OF REUBEN KENISTON, LEACH FAMILY BURIAL GROUND, ELLIOTT STREET, DANVERS. The 24-year-old Beverly minuteman who fell on what is now celebrated as Patriots' Day, was interred, probably with relatives, in the small graveyard that was then a part of Beverly. It is located to the right of Folly Hill Farm.

PALLADIUM OF BOSTON, HENRY LARCOM COMMANDER (EARLY-19TH-CENTURY WATERCOLOR). The *Palladium* was not a "privateer"—a privately owned vessel commissioned to attack, capture, and take spoils during wartime. However, one of the first privateers to sail from Beverly Harbor in 1776 during the Revolutionary War was the brigantine *Washington*, which was named to honor the first general of the Continental Army. After the war, imports again became an important part of ocean-borne commerce. Between April 1 and July 1, 1787, the town imported about 3,100 gallons of foreign rum, 7,000 gallons of "other foreign distilled spirits," 400 pounds of cocoa, 3,500 pounds of sugar (sweetening for the popular beverage tea), and 50,000 pounds of leaf tobacco (to be stuffed into white clay pipes). (Photograph courtesy Ronald Bourgeault, Northeast Auctions.)

"THE NEW POWDER HOUSE," OFF MADISON AVENUE ON PROSPECT HILL (C. 1906 POSTCARD). Early arsenals, including the ones in Marblehead and Newburyport, were built of brick and were round or octagonal, such as this 1808 structure. They are visual reminders of past efforts to keep a town's powder dry in case of a local or national emergency. Beverly's "old" powderhouse was built on the south side of the common in 1767. (Courtesy Clayton Collection.)

THE CAPT. HUGH HILL HOUSE, 50 FRONT STREET. A cousin of Andrew Jackson (the seventh president of the United States), Hugh Hill emigrated from Ireland, where he had been born in 1740 in Carrickfergus. Due to Captain Hill's privateering luck and pluck—and that of other Beverlyites such as Benjamin Ellingwood, Eleazer Giles, and Jacob Oliver—the Continental Army became supplied with British goods and occasionally gold. This enabled it to defeat King George III's army and thus become separate from the mother country. Hugh Hill is the main character in the 1967 novel *Fish Flake Hill*, where his *c.* 1780 Georgian mansion sits prominently among its architectural neighbors. (Courtesy William Finch and Carol Rose.)

CAPT. JOHN THISSEL (C. 1800 OIL ON CANVAS BY AN UNIDENTIFIED ARTIST). A well-dressed portly gentleman, Captain Thissel was the son of John and Lucy (Lovett) Thissel. In 1797, he took Rebecca Ober to be his wife. While visiting St. Lucia in the West Indies in 1809, he died at the age of 36 years. (Courtesy Mr. and Mrs. Paul Zaido; photograph courtesy Marine Art Gallery.)

Two

THE CITY PROPER

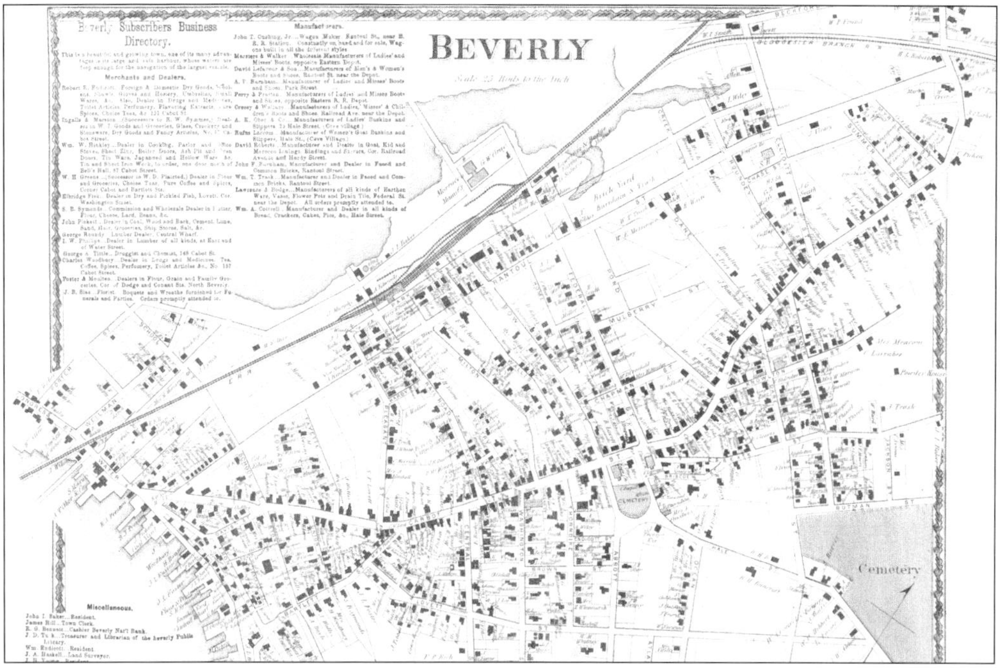

A MAP OF BEVERLY (1872). In 1802, the Reverend Dr. William Bentley, pastor of the East Church in neighboring Salem, noted in his diary that Beverly had "an old Meeting house & a few scattered houses . . . on the great road [then called Main Street, now Cabot Street], with all the appearances of a farming town in the memory of the present generation. The brick & elegant Houses [depicted in red on maps] have all been built since I came to Salem & since I preached at Beverly. The Wharves have been put into an entirely new condition." After mentioning two mansion houses with which he was familiar, Dr. Bentley closed the entry in his diary by writing that "most of the old buildings have been taken away." Fortunately, the oldest wood-framed dwelling in New England, the John Balch House at 448 Cabot Street (see p. 36), did not meet the fate that the pastor-antiquarian described. As noted on this map, most of the city's residences and businesses were clustered around Carbot Street (*sic*) in the late 19th century.

ABBOTT STREET, LOOKING EAST FROM MONUMENT SQUARE (1900 POSTCARD). Located off Cabot Street, Abbott Street is parallel to and between Thorndike and Ocean Streets. At a town meeting in August 1868, it was accepted to extend Abbott Street over the Old Burial Ground and to establish it permanently as a town way. The remains of many early residents were reinterred on the other side of the street along with their sandstone or slate grave stones. (Courtesy Beverly Public Library.)

ATLANTIC AVENUE, NEAR THE CORNER OF HALE STREET (EARLY-20TH-CENTURY POSTCARD). The First Church of Christ Scientist, Beverly, is now located at the left corner of the avenue, which has a perspective view to the ocean.

A View on Broadway (1893 Photograph). The wood-framed, Queen Anne house (left) on the thoroughfare's downward slope somewhat mimics the high Victorian brick Odd Fellows' Hall on the corner of Cabot Street. (Courtesy Beverly Public Library.)

BROADWAY LOOKING WEST TOWARD RYAL SIDE (C. 1895 POSTCARD). Turreted, mansard, and gabled slate roofs on well-to-do Broadway contrast with the semicircular roof of Beverly's second train station, located on Park Street. The Bass River in the background separates the city proper from rural Ryal Side with its randomly sited homes and farmhouses. (Courtesy Beverly Public Library.)

THE ENDICOTT-GALE HOUSE, 16 BROADWAY (EARLY-20TH-CENTURY POSTCARD). Creeping ivy camouflages the variegated, ocher-colored brick facade of the Colonial Revival mansion, which features a Palladian window in the projecting pavilion and a welcoming semicircular portico with a classical balustrade. Dr. and Mrs. Charles Howard Gale were residents there during the second quarter of the 20th century; he was a well-respected minister, college professor, and gynecologist. (Courtesy Beverly Public Library.)

ROWAND'S, 2 CABOT STREET (C. 1975 PHOTOGRAPH). Capt. William Stopford, who owned the brick townhouse on this site, also operated a fish market and the North Shore Lobster Company, which he sold to F. Elliott Rowand in 1959. Rowand's first building was brought to this site on a barge from Manchester-by-the-Sea in the early 1920s, and the present building was erected in 1981. (Courtesy F. Elliott and Dave Rowand.)

THE COLONIAL DINER, 4 CABOT STREET (C. 1940S PHOTOGRAPH). The French-Canadian firm incorporated as the Worcester Lunch Car Company manufactured this cream- and green-painted diner (No. 733) and delivered it to the proud French-Canadian owners in 1937. Charles LeClerc and Ralph Cloutier were pleased with their newspaper advertisement: "Whether you are in the mood for a light snack or a full course dinner you will surely enjoy your stop at the Colonial Diner, one of the finest modern dining establishments on the entire North Shore." (Courtesy Rowand Collection.)

Cabot Street from the Essex Bridge (c. 1911 Postcard). Approaching the bridge to Salem, a horse-drawn trolley passes an early-18th-century, gambrel-roofed dwelling. Captain Stopford's brick townhouse is at the far left, and not visible at the right is the four-story brick factory building at the intersection of Rantoul (left) and Cabot Streets. The Frost Box Company, incorporated in 1908, occupied that building, which was on the site of the Atlantic House Hotel, a Greek Revival–style structure that burned in 1851. (Courtesy Beverly Public Library.)

Cabot Street from Edwards Street (c. 1900 Postcard). Edwards Street is the second one from the wedge-shaped corner of Rantoul and Cabot Streets. It was named for Col. Abraham Edwards, whose residence was located midway on that street and whose name is perpetuated on the 1912 brick grammar school on the corner of Rantoul Street. In 1839, artist-author John Warner Barber wrote that Beverly "is a large village, mostly built on a single street," which was called Main Street at that time. (Courtesy Beverly Public Library.)

CABOT STREET FROM THE CORNER OF FAYETTE STREET (C. 1900 POSTCARD). Two Federal-period dwellings on the left side of the street (each with a hipped roof and tall chimneys) repose near a Queen Anne–style "cottage" with its various architectural variations and tower. The Greek Revival–style house, owned by John Pickett, a coal and wood dealer in the 1870s, is on the other side of Cabot Street at the far right. Although the house next to the corner one at 68 Fayette Street is gone, the substantial brick Federal-period house with first-floor shop windows stands today at the corner of May Street. Ebenezer Lovett, a bricklayer who resided at 153 Hale Street in Beverly Cove, may have had a hand in the construction of the Federal-period building. (Courtesy Beverly Public Library.)

CABOT STREET LOOKING WEST FROM THE CORNER OF HIGHLAND AVENUE (C. 1900 POSTCARD). Snow-covered branches of feathery trees glisten in the afternoon sun while the city's houses and streets show the aftermath of a sizable winter storm. On January 18, 1904, thermometers showed the temperature to be 19 degrees below zero. On January 27, electric car service was curtailed by another winter storm. (Courtesy Beverly Public Library.)

THE BEVERLY HISTORICAL SOCIETY AND MUSEUM, 117 CABOT STREET (1905 POSTCARD). Built in 1781 for merchant John Cabot, the Georgian-style brick building retains its original molded roof cornice and string courses (which define the stories), but has a later Greek Revival front doorway and a still later Victorian cast-iron fence. In 1891, when the historical society was organized, it acquired the Cabot House, which had been the first home of the Beverly Bank between 1802 and 1868. Period furniture and furnishings are displayed in formal and informal rooms, and changing exhibits highlight aspects of the city's rich past. The Laurence Breed Walker Transportation Collection is an adjunct of the historical society and is open on Wednesday evenings.

CABOT STREET FROM THE CORNER OF CENTRAL STREET (C. 1900 POSTCARD). Long-gone trees soar above the Beverly Historical Society and Museum (far right) as well as the small, 18th-century house on the corner of Franklin Place and the Victorian, wood-framed business blocks that have sprung up in the center of the city. Striped awnings and various trade signs on the large, now-vanished 1883 Commercial Block building vie for the attention of passers-by out on errands. In 1909, the Beverly and Danvers Street Railway became part of the Lynn and Boston railway system.

A MILLINERY AND FANCY GOODS TRADE CARD (C. 1890). Mesdames Allen & Pickett served the needs of the town's consumers. Some other retailers and service-oriented businesses on Cabot Street in 1893 included the following: Hiram Kimball Jr., a practical electrician (No. 92); Dr. E.B. Dudley, a dentist who specialized in "carved teeth" (No. 107); Henry L. Green, an apothecary and chemist (No. 128); J.A. Wilson, "the leading stationer" (No. 146); Lombard & Dunn, fashionable milliners and dealers in goods and novelties (No. 207); and H.W. Gould, who sold cigars and smokers' articles (No. 134).

Cabot Street from the Corner of Milton Street (c. 1900 Postcard). The buildings on the sunny side of the street include, from left to right, the following: the 1883 Commercial Block building; the mansard-roof structure (No. 146) that was the location of Kennedy & Company, the popular butter-and-egg store; a building (No. 150) that looks as if it might have been raised one story; the Peabody Building (No. 156), built of brick and terra-cotta in 1890; and the two abutting brick and granite buildings (Nos. 160 and 162). Pewterer Israel Trask had a shop in the left structure between 1812 and 1840. He and his brothers, George and Oliver, as well as fellow pewterers, Eben Smith and Philip Lee, are especially regarded today for their lighthouse-style coffeepots with bright-cut decoration made of Brittania, an alloy of pewter.

CABOT STREET FROM THE INTERSECTION OF BROADWAY (LEFT) AND THORNDIKE STREET (C. 1895 POSTCARD). The main commercial street in the city was named for the brothers Cabot, who moved to Beverly in 1771 and who soon became prominent patriots, citizens, and merchants. A contemporary merchant, Robert Rantoul, opened the first apothecary shop in America in 1796 nearby, at the corner of Cabot and Washington Streets.

The Odd Fellows' Hall, 188–194 Cabot Street (Early-20th-Century Postcard). The wrought-iron weathervane that surmounts the 1875 brick structure and the carved limestone plaque on the facade bear masonic symbols known to those who practice the craft. There were many secret and benevolent societies in Beverly during the late 19th and early 20th centuries. Some had fascinating names: Amity Royal Arch Chapter; Benevolent Order of Buffaloes, No. 6; Chickataubut Tribe, No. 13; Consort Lodge; Degree of Pocahontas; Knights Templar, St. George Commandery; Penny Aid; and Mizpah Commandery, No. 283.

Klink's Bakery, 143 Cabot Street (1895 Photograph). With folded arms, Carl Klink Sr. poses in front of his first shop, which features a snow-white frosted Christmas castle in the display window. Klink put the finishing touches and the flags on the confectionery creation with the assistance of three employees. A sign in the window by the electrical wiring lets passers-by know they may purchase Vienna bread. A candy sign on the building's corner advertises homemade molasses candy. (Courtesy Durrell Collection.)

The Production Floor of Klink's Bakery, 255 Cabot Street (c. 1922 Photograph). Traces of flour on the floor, the wooden barrels, and the imagined fragrance of baking bread and other goods adds to the interest of this image. Carl Klink Sr. stands by the open oven door while his namesake stands with arms akimbo by a dough trough on wheels. Another baker in the city was George C. Stickney, who resided in the 1880 house at 55 Hale Street. (Courtesy Durrell Collection.)

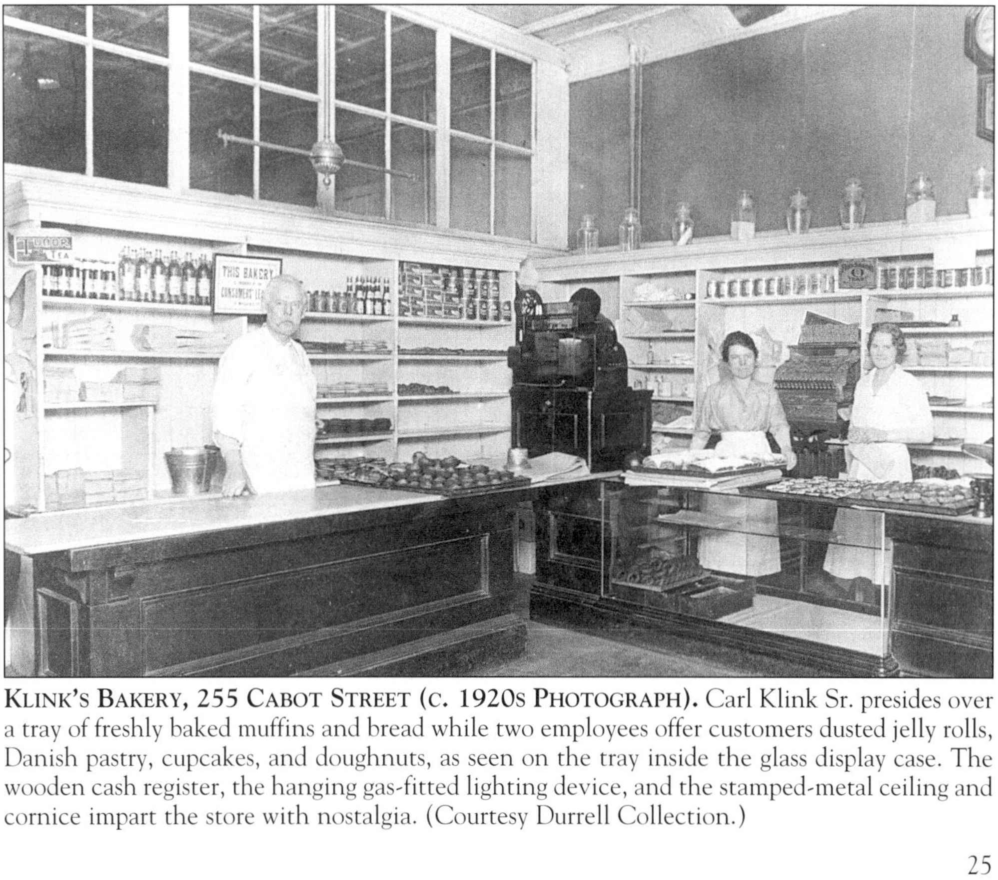

Klink's Bakery, 255 Cabot Street (c. 1920s Photograph). Carl Klink Sr. presides over a tray of freshly baked muffins and bread while two employees offer customers dusted jelly rolls, Danish pastry, cupcakes, and doughnuts, as seen on the tray inside the glass display case. The wooden cash register, the hanging gas-fitted lighting device, and the stamped-metal ceiling and cornice impart the store with nostalgia. (Courtesy Durrell Collection.)

THE CITY HALL, 191 CABOT STREET (1905 POSTCARD). Unsightly utility poles detract from this view of Andrew Cabot's former brick mansion, which had received a third story with a mansard roof in 1874. Pres. James Monroe had been entertained there during Cabot's ownership, and the building was first used as a town hall in 1841. In 1933–1934, while the Honorable Paul S. Eaton was mayor, the top story was removed as a WPA project, so the building appears much as it did when built in 1785.

"BEVERLY'S FINEST" (C. 1885 PHOTOGRAPH). Seventeen members of the police force, including George T. Larcom (standing fourth from the right), pose for an official city picture. Other constables on the force in 1885 were George Clark, Benjamin F. Herrick, Chester Hobbs, George E. Johnson, John G. Munsey, and William Stevens. The white-bearded gentleman seated in the front row is probably William Woodbury, the chief of police. (Courtesy Clayton Collection.)

MANUEL'S BLACK AND WHITE ORCHESTRA (C. 1949 PHOTOGRAPH). The Manuel family moved to the Garden City c. 1900. They began performing before World War I as Manuel's Original Orchestra, with founders Otis and Dave on the trumpet and trombone respectively and "Aunt Cindy" on the bass. The six white musicians in the group gave it the distinction of being the first integrated band (and the oldest continuously playing one) in the nation. Shown, from left to right, are Tony Pappa, Otis Manuel, Matt Carrington, Peter Alleruzzo, Charlie Manuel, Alvin Mitchell, and Dave Manuel. (Courtesy Alvin Mitchell.)

A MEMORIAL DAY PARADE ALONG CABOT STREET (C. 1920S PHOTOGRAPH). Bystanders line the city's main commercial thoroughfare at the corners of Wallis (foreground) and Thorndike Streets. Younger marchers precede older dignitaries, who are spared the length of the parade. (Courtesy Robert W. Atherton.)

THE FIRST BAPTIST CHURCH IN BEVERLY, 221 CABOT STREET (C. 1900 PHOTOGRAPH). One of the city's prominent landmarks is the architecturally interesting and multifaceted steeple of this religious edifice, built in 1801. (Courtesy First Baptist Church in Beverly.)

THE WOMEN'S SOCIETY OF THE FIRST BAPTIST CHURCH PREPARE CHRISTMAS GIFTS FOR A KODIAK, ALASKA MISSION (C. 1960S PHOTOGRAPH). Church ladies decorate trees with handmade mittens and gifts for less fortunate people in their outreach missionary program. The volunteers include, from left to right, Betty Clark, Roz Cole Little, Doris Cole, and Sandy Sparks Hiram (wife of Rev. David Hiram). (Courtesy First Baptist Church in Beverly.)

"C.L. DODGE AS SANTA AT BAPTIST CHURCH ABOUT 1871." Looking more like a wizard than old St. Nick, this elderly gentleman is shown in a previously unpublished ferrotype (tintype) that may be one of the earliest photographic representations of Santa Claus as imagined by New York cartoonist Thomas Nast around that time. (Courtesy First Baptist Church in Beverly.)

Conflagration at the First Baptist Church in Beverly, 221 Cabot Street (August 26, 1975 Photograph). Black smoke emanates from the white-painted church during the general-alarm fire that destroyed the building, but fortunately not the steeple. (Courtesy Atherton Collection.)

Cabot Street at Ellis Square (c. 1925 Postcard). This busy intersection was named to honor H. Gordon Ellis, a World War I veteran. The ornate commercial Beverly Building at the far right was designed by Henry Bailey Alden. It stood on the site of the addition to the First Baptist church. Steeples of the First Parish Unitarian church and of St. Mary's Star of the Sea Church dominate the city skyline, with those of the Briscoe School on Essex Street in the right background. Goodwin's (center) had counter service and was where locals enjoyed "lunch at the bus stop." Other popular midday eateries included the Miss Beverly Diner at 386 Cabot Street, advertised as "the smart place to dine"; Ropes Drug Store in the Odd Fellows' Block, serving "fountain luncheons"; and F.W. Woolworth & Company at 234 Cabot Street, offering "luncheon and fountain specials." (Courtesy Beverly Public Library.)

The First Parish Unitarian Church, 225 Cabot Street (1905 Postcard). Beverly's first meetinghouse was built in 1656. The First Parish Unitarian Church was organized on September 20, 1667, with the Reverend John Hale as the flock's first pastor. This chaste, Greek Revival structure features the date 1667 in the roundel on the steeple above four carved decorative laurel wreaths.

The YMCA, 245 Cabot Street (c. 1925 Postcard). The most important personage in America and in Beverly during the summer of 1910 was Pres. William Howard Taft, who laid the cornerstone for this building on the last day of August. In 1968, during Beverly's tercentenary, it was noted that the YMCA was "literally 'bursting at the seams,' as young and older men and women seek physical exercise for health and enjoyment." That same year, Laurie Richards (age 14) and Gary Peterson (age 13) were honored as the YMCA's girl and boy of the year.

Nutter's Beverly Shop, 248A Cabot Street (c. 1942 Photograph). Mima S. Dallas, the treasurer and manager of the small dry goods store (and secretary of the Beverly School Department), surveys customers while Arthur C. Cressy Sr., the assistant manager and window dresser, stands at the cash register. Local ladies purchased their hosiery and household items at "the home of Kenwood Blankets." They also stocked "drapery material, curtains, lingerie, and domestics." (Courtesy Arthur Cheever Cressy Jr.)

ST. MARY'S STAR OF THE SEA CHURCH, 251 CABOT STREET (C. 1909 POSTCARD). Built in 1908, two years before the YMCA, the brick and sandstone Romanesque church features impressive stained-glass windows and an imposing bell tower. A carved and gilded inscription at sidewalk level reads, "1897 S·Maria·Maris·Stella." The construction date appears on the right side of the front entranceway.

President Taft's Executive Office, Corner of Cabot and Federal Streets (c. 1910 Postcard). When in residence at the summer White House (see chapter 5), President Taft maintained offices on the second floor of this building above the Almy, Bigelow & Washburn department store. The Beverly National Bank purchased the property in 1920 and occupied space in the building, which was destroyed by fire in 1958.

Cabot Street at the Intersection of West Dane (Left) and Dane Streets (c. 1905 Postcard). Trees in summer's full leafage partially obscure houses on both sides of the mainly residential street, with the only recognizable landmark being the Dutch gambrel-roofed building with the first-floor grocery store of Hatch and Mitchell near the corner of West Dane Street. Farther along, and on the opposite side of Cabot Street at 337, is the 1696 dwelling built by house carpenter Hazadiah Smith. Souvenir postcards of Beverly were sold for 10¢ per set in 1900 by John B. Webb, the jeweler at 45 Cabot Street. (Courtesy Beverly Public Library.)

LE GRAND DAVID AND HIS OWN SPECTACULAR MAGIC COMPANY, 286 CABOT STREET. This extravagant, classic-style magic show continues to offer joy, mirth, and amazement a quarter century after its 1977 debut at the 1920s-vintage Cabot Street Cinema Theatre. (Courtesy White Horse Productions.)

THE JOHN BALCH HOUSE, 448 CABOT STREET (C. 1970S POSTCARD). The house that William Woodberry built in 1630 may have been the first dwelling erected in Beverly. The first land grant was authorized five years later to five of the "Old Planters," one of whom, John Balch, built the earliest part of the lean-to (saltbox) house that is so venerated by architectural historians and Balch family members. A significant First Period dwelling, the *c.* 1636 house is on the corner of Balch Street, which leads to the "Planters' Path," where the first landing occurred on the Bass River.

A BEVERLY TERCENTENARY PROGRAM (JUNE, 1930). Although Beverly was founded in 1626, a tercentenary was held in 1930, when Roy K. Patch was mayor. Historical highlights included a meeting in the auditorium of the new high school and automobile trips to cultural sights. A tercentenary dinner was held at the city hall one evening, followed by a parade the next day and fireworks that night at the Athletic Association Field of the United Shoe Machinery Corporation. (Courtesy Cressy Collection.)

The Gove Lumber Company's Delivery Truck, 80 Colon Street (c. 1920s Photograph). Founded in 1910 by brothers George A. and Charles E. Gove Jr., the company sold lumber and building materials, including doors, hardware, blinds, and sash. Records indicate that a quantity of hemlock and spruce boards, red cedar clapboards, and plain pine planking was sold to a Miss B.P. Parshley of Beverly in September 1915 for $172.55. Getting ready for such a delivery are Walter Davey (leaning on the lumber), a cousin of Robert H. Gove, and Edwin Gove, another cousin. (Courtesy Robert W. Gove.)

An Employees' Dinner Party (c. 1956 Photograph). Several valued people on the staff of the Gove Lumber Company were treated to dinner and drinks on this special occasion. Clockwise from the back corner are Joe Nuccio, the husband of bookkeeper Mary Nuccio, seated next to him; Ellen Englehardt, another keeper of the books; Mrs. Leo Pariseau and her husband, who was a truck driver; George Moore and his wife, Barbara, a third bookkeeper; and Walter Englehardt, who accompanied his wife for the evening out. (Courtesy Gove Collection.)

The Dane Street Congregational Church, Corner of Dane and Knowlton Streets (Early-19th-Century Wood Engraving). Dedicated on April 1, 1803, the 64-foot-long by 50-foot-wide meetinghouse had 12-over-12 window sash and an entrance in the stair tower, which was 20 feet above the roofline. In 1815, when Rev. Joseph Emerson may have still been the pastor, a 1,143-ton bronze bell was installed. The bell may have been salvaged from the fire that destroyed the house of worship in 1832. (Courtesy private collection.)

The Bath Pavilion at Dane Street Beach (c. 1920s Postcard). An American flag flutters in the breeze on a sunny afternoon as people stroll on the grounds surrounding the neoclassical-style pavilion. The park there is referred to as Dane Street Beach, Oceanside Park, and the Percy F. Lyons Park.

A DELIGHTFUL DAY AT DANE STREET BEACH (C. 1905 POSTCARD). Several women holding black parasols, little girls with white hair ribbons, and men wearing assorted headgear enjoy carefree hours by the crescent-shaped beach. (Courtesy Clayton Collection.)

LOOKING OUT TO SEA (C. 1940 PHOTOGRAPH). Ryal Side residents Paul S. Larcom and his Swedish-born mother, Ingrid Svendsen, gaze out to sea. Sidney Larcom, the head custodian of the Dane Street Bath House for many years, sits contentedly on the side of the lifeguard's dory, perhaps wishing he could be out sailing a larger version of the ship model he is holding. (Courtesy Paul S. Larcom.)

THE BRISCOE SCHOOL, 3 ESSEX STREET NEAR THE INTERSECTION OF BRISCOE STREET (C. 1910 POSTCARD). Built of brick and limestone on a knoll behind Cabot Street, the high Victorian structure had a mansard roof, stair tower, and a patterned slate roof before a fire destroyed the interior and roof in 1996. The name of the city's first high school and its dates are carved over the ecclesiastical-shaped front entrance: "Briscoe School 1674 / 1874." The first date pertains to the year the town selectmen voted to build a schoolhouse.

THE HARDIE SCHOOL, 23 ESSEX STREET (EARLY-20TH-CENTURY POSTCARD). The brick grammar school that now looks upon the recently restored Beverly Common of 1705, was named to honor Samuel Hardie, the town's first schoolmaster. In 1915, the principal was Clara A. Smith. She and 12 other women, most of whom were probably unmarried, taught students in the first eight grades. The Montserrat College of Art, a four-year accredited institution, has occupied the former grammar school since 1992. (Courtesy Beverly Public Library.)

THE BEVERLY PUBLIC LIBRARY, 32 ESSEX STREET (C. 1915 POSTCARD). Established elsewhere in 1855 to be "free to all," the public library moved into its present building between Winter (left) and Dane Streets in 1913. Paid for by the city, the brick, marble, and limestone Beaux Arts structure was designed by Cass Gilbert, who was the architect of the Woolworth Building in New York City. The names of local authors and poets grace the front and two sides of the library in tablets between the cornice and windows. An architecturally appealing addition in 1993 provided more space for books and their browsers.

DAWN (C. 1975 DRAWING ON PAPER BY WILL BARNET). Beverly's most famous native son, Will Barnet, was born in 1911. He lives in New York City and is regarded as a leading American modernist. Barnet donated many of his visually striking prints to the Beverly Public Library, and they are on view in the lower level gallery that bears his name. (Courtesy Will Barnet.)

A SIMPLE DWELLING ON FISH FLAKE HILL, 31 FRONT STREET (1905 POSTCARD). Around 21 historic 18th- and 19th-century buildings are located on Fish Flake Hill—the area between Front and Water Streets that was once covered with fish flake yards. The house shown no longer exists. However, set back from 41 Front Street (the 18th-century Herrick Tavern) is the former West Farms School of 1780, which became the first high school in 1859.

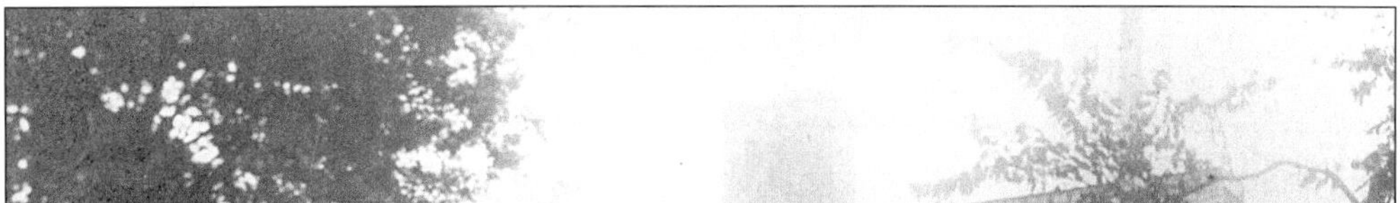

THE CAPT. JOSIAH BATCHELDER JR. HOUSE, 22 FRONT STREET (EARLY-20TH-CENTURY POSTCARD). This historic gambrel-roof dwelling was where Hannah Hill and Joanna Batchelder Prince taught the first Sunday school classes in America in 1810. The young women taught the principles of Christian living to about 30 wayward youngsters for many Sundays. (Courtesy Beverly Public Library.)

A Fish Flake Hill Preservation Battle (1970 Newspaper Photograph). Dan Campbell, director of the Beverly Historical Development Foundation (shown in the window of the left frame), tried to forestall Police Chief Edward Aucone from demolishing the Capt. Hugh Hill family home. His efforts on behalf of the foundation were unsuccessful, and the c. 1784 Front Street house was razed. It is shown at right just before being demolished.

The Capt. Robert Briscoe Warehouse, 1 Front Street. Located at the V-shaped intersection of Water Street, this *c.* 1703 building may be the oldest surviving business building in America. (Courtesy Finch and Rose Collection.)

A PORTRAIT OF THE GASTONGUAY FAMILY (1935 PHOTOGRAPH). French Canadians Joseph and Marie Gastonguay, who moved to Beverly from Livermore Falls, Maine, resided in a three-decker on Grant Street with their 11 children. The brood included Emilie and Regina (seated) as well as Blanche, Emil, Arthur, Wilfred, George, Alfred, Hervie, Hector, and Elmina. A few French Huguenot refugees arrived in Beverly before the end of the 17th century, bearing names such as Auber, LaCombe, and LeFevre, which became Anglicized and carried on by their descendants as Ober, Larcom, and Lefavour respectively. Some French-Canadian families emigrated to Beverly around the Civil War period, while the Gastonguays arrived in the first decade of the 20th century. (Courtesy Rita St. Pierre.)

LES PETITES ST. PIERRES (C. 1930 PHOTOGRAPH). Four of Arthur and Elmina St. Pierre's children—Annette, Rita, Roger, and baby Laura—wait outside their "grandmere's" three-decker to be taken for ice-cream cones. They all attended the grammar school at St. Alphonse's Church, which was located at 40 Railroad Avenue. The three-deckers on one side of Simon Street were ready for occupancy by USM families by 1912. (Courtesy St. Pierre Collection.)

THE CENTRAL FIRE STATION, 15 HALE STREET (C. 1920S POSTCARD). The thin, wooden steeple of the First Baptist church appears in the background. The brick fire station, with its substantial hose-drying tower and three-door facade, was built in 1884. In the late 19th and early 20th centuries, the station housed Steamer No. 1, Hook & Ladder No. 2, and Steamer No. 2. Around the turn of the century, there were 31 fire alarm boxes in the city, with nonsequential numbers. By 1915, there were 77 fire alarm boxes, including those in North Beverly and Beverly Farms. The alarm was tested daily at 11:45 with one blast; two blasts indicated that the fire had been extinguished; three blasts was a call for more hose; four blasts prompted the second steamer to arrive at the conflagration; and three repeated blasts indicated that the fire was out of town.

LADDER NO. 2, CENTRAL FIRE STATION, 15 HALE STREET. In 1915, when Engines No. 1 and No. 2 were located in the Central Fire Station, William A. Richardson was the captain and William L. Colson was the first lieutenant. (Courtesy Atherton Collection.)

HALE STREET NEAR THE CORNER OF MONUMENT SQUARE, (EARLY-20TH-CENTURY POSTCARD). Not visible at the far left is the 18th-century, gambrel-roof residence of Col. Larkin Thorndike at 16–18 Hale Street. A house plaque indicates that he was "Captain of the Minutemen, 1775." The house with the cupola on Hale Street was known as the Swasey House, and the *c.* 1785 house at 21–23 Hale Street features a hipped roof and enclosed porticoes.

THE HALE FARM, HALE STREET (1892 PHOTOGRAPH BY FRANK COUSINS). The 1695 dwelling where Rev. John Hale's family resided is the steeply pitched section (not visible) behind the large mid-18th-century addition, now devoid of the pronounced portico. U-shaped Bancroft Avenue surrounds the spacious property, which was purchased from family descendants in 1938 by the Beverly Historical Society. (Courtesy Schier Collection.)

The Gravestone of Rev. John Hale (1636–1700), Old Burial Ground, Abbott Street. Chosen as pastor of the First Church in Beverly in 1667, the Reverend Mr. Hale shepherded his flock for more than 30 years. He was regarded as "a pious and faithful minister of ye gospel," even though he was an early instigator of the 1692 witchcraft trials in Salem. Two years after that episode ended, he had the house at Hale Street built (possibly with architectural elements from an earlier parsonage), where he lived for five more years until passing on to his reward.

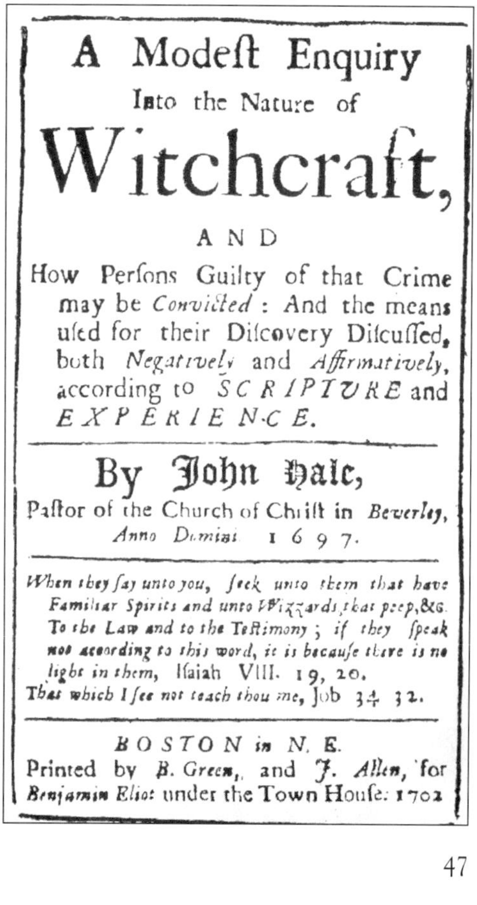

A Modeſt Enquiry
Into the Nature of
Witchcraft,
AND
How Perſons Guilty of that Crime may be *Convicted* : And the means uſed for their Diſcovery Diſcuſſed, both *Negatively* and *Affirmatively*, according to *SCRIPTURE* and *EXPERIENCE.*

By John Hale,
Paſtor of the Church of Chriſt in *Beverley*,
Anno Domini 1697.

When they ſay unto you, ſeek unto them that have Familiar Spirits and unto Wizzards, that peep, &c. *To the Law and to the Teſtimony ; if they ſpeak not according to this word, it is becauſe there is no light in them*, Iſaiah VIII. 19, 20.
That which I ſee not teach thou me, Job 34. 32.

BOSTON in N. E.
Printed by *B. Green*, and *J. Allen*, for *Benjamin Eliot* under the Town Houſe: 1702

A *Modest Enquiry*, (1697 Title Page of a Small Book, Written by Rev. John Hale and Published Posthumously in 1702). An eyewitness to many of the diabolical events occurring in Salem Village and Salem Town in 1692, the Reverend Mr. Hale wanted to record the facts, as he remembered them, for posterity. He had no doubt that witchcraft was being practiced locally and later realized (after his wife, Sarah, had been falsely accused in early November) that he, the magistrates, and others were terribly wrong in their judgment of the 20 victims. (Courtesy private collection.)

THE BEVERLY HOSPITAL, HERRICK STREET (EARLY-20TH-CENTURY POSTCARD). Land that the hospital's corporation acquired in 1906 on Herrick and Heather Streets became the site of the new building, which was dedicated and opened on September 8, 1908. In 1915, some of the hospital's officers, who were elected annually in June, included John L. Saltonstall, president; Roland W. Boyden, secretary; and Augustus P. Loring, treasurer. Some specialists on the staff included G.A. Stickney, M.D., obstetrician; Ralph E. Stone, M.D., anesthetist; C.W. Haddock, M.D., eye, ear, and throat; and O.F. Swasey, M.D., a consulting physician.

THE QUEEN HOTEL, 37 LOTHROP STREET (C. 1889 PHOTOGRAPH BY FRANK COUSINS). Probably named for Queen Victoria, the Shingle-style, turreted hostelry was opened to the public in June 1889, with Israel Lefavour as proprietor. An advertisement claimed that it was "delightfully located on the Beverly Shore. Handsomely furnished and provided with modern improvements. Superior facilities for boating and bathing." Shortly thereafter, on November 24, 1891, fire destroyed the spacious hotel with an estimated loss of $75,000. The choice oceanside lot on which the hotel stood became the property of the city in 1906. (Courtesy Schier Collection.)

THE DINING ROOM IN THE QUEEN HOTEL, 37 LOTHROP STREET (C. 1889 PHOTOGRAPH BY FRANK COUSINS). Fan and fluted white linen napkins grace the tables in the dining room with its patterned ceiling, stenciled cornice, and curiously draped gas chandeliers. Such commodities as beef, lamb, poultry, butter, and "Hampden Cream" may have been supplied by Larcom, Bell & Company, which was located at 98 Cabot Street around the turn of the century. Known for their "fine groceries," the firm also offered "table luxuries" for their well-to-do customers. (Courtesy Schier Collection.)

QUEEN BEACH, LOTHROP STREET (EARLY-20TH-CENTURY POSTCARD). Referred to by its regal name for many years after the hotel was gone, the area provided beachgoers and sightseers with a wonderful view of Beverly Harbor and Salem Willows (far left), an amusement park at the tip of what was then beginning to be known as the "Witch City."

INDEPENDENCE PARK, LOTHROP STREET (EARLY-20TH-CENTURY POSTCARD). On March 13, 1907, Independence Park became the official name given to the lot of land where part of the Queen Hotel was located. A bronze plaque (inset in a boulder in 1929 by the Col. Ebenezer Francis Chapter, Daughters of the American Revolution) commemorates two historic events that took place there. On September 5, 1775, John Glover's vessel, the *Hannah*, sailed forth from that location, and on July 17, 1776, he read the Declaration of Independence to local troops. In past years, band concerts and fireworks were enjoyed by all at Independence Park, which is one of four waterfront parks in the city.

ALONG LOTHROP STREET BY INDEPENDENCE PARK (EARLY-20TH-CENTURY POSTCARD). The occupants of the houses opposite the sloping park and those in the Italianate-style house (at the right with the stair tower) have remarkable views of the harbor and many of the islands in the distance.

STROMBERG'S, 126 LOTHROP STREET (C. 1941 POSTCARD). Hungry and thirsty beachgoers would line up at this popular fast-food restaurant directly opposite the Dane Street Bath House for take-out orders of hamburgers, hot dogs, french fries, and tonic. Sharpy's Sea Breeze, also located in the area, was where people could enjoy "good food at the beach." (Courtesy Beverly Public Library.)

SOME POLITE PICKETERS WALKING BY THE IDEAL SUPPLY COMPANY, 47 MILL STREET (C. 1920S PHOTOGRAPH). One of the most acrimonious strikes in the city's history occurred on March 5, 1920, when some 3,000 USM machinists, about half of the Beverly plant's entire labor force, walked off the job. Led by Local 348 Pres. Charles W. Fitzgerald, organizer William H. Larkin, and other union officials, the action was in protest against alleged company coercion of employee contracts. Despite efforts at mediation by the U.S. Labor Department, the strike continued through the spring until workers were finally forced back to their jobs by the Massachusetts Supreme Court. (Courtesy St. Pierre Collection.)

THE CIVIL WAR MONUMENT, MONUMENT SQUARE (1905 POSTCARD). One of the most imposing granite memorials in Essex County relating to the War Between the States is this one located adjacent to the Old Burial Ground where Abbott, Endicott, and Hale Streets meet. Inscriptions on four sides of the plinth relate, "To the soldiers and sailors of Beverly [who by] teaching in eloquent silence the lesson of the citizen's duty to the state [are] embalmed in the memories of succeeding generations, the heroic dead will live on in immortal youth . . . erected on behalf of the citizens of the town of Beverly by Post 89, Dept., of Mass., Grand Army of the Republic, 1882."

THE BOSTON AND MAINE RAILROAD STATION, PARK STREET (EARLY-20TH-CENTURY POSTCARD). The third railroad station at this location is an ocher-colored, brick Richardsonian-style structure with brownstone trim. Situated on the westerly side of the tracks, the 116- by 32-foot building was designed by Bradford Lee Gilbert and was opened for travelers in September 1897. Odell Park, Depot Square, and Rantoul Square are synonymous names used to identify the park in front of the depot that is flanked by Railroad Avenue and Broadway. The shoe manufacturing firm of Perry & Wood was located in the wood-framed building with corner quoins, seen through the outbound passenger waiting area. (Courtesy Beverly Public Library.)

A Panorama of the Beverly Depot (c. 1900 Postcard). Brick factories and wood-framed businesses of different sizes located in the immediate area between Park and Rantoul Streets are on the right side of the image. The circular brick gas works building is a visible landmark at the left, along with other structures next to the Bass River. (Courtesy Gary Thomas.)

"Riding the Rails" (c. 1890 Photograph). Joseph H. Cressy holds the pump handle of the hand car and is probably responsible for the brake as well. His son, Arthur C. Cressy Sr., is to his right. The other employees of the Boston and Maine Railroad and the boy are unidentified. (Courtesy Cressy Collection.)

THE JOSEPH H. CRESSY FAMILY, 13 PHILLIPS COURT (C. 1890 PHOTOGRAPH). As the breadwinner of this large family, Joseph H. Cressy was a section foreman with the Boston and Maine Railroad in the 1890s. Shown, from left to right, the Cressy family members are Arthur, Clara, Walter, Agnes, Fred (Agnes's husband), baby Austin, Clara Stevens Cressy (Joseph's wife), Joseph, Mabel Frances, and twin Nellie. Nellie Cressy was drowned when the 75-ton excursion steamboat *Surf City* partially capsized on Beverly Bar. Travelling a triangular route between Beverly, Salem Willows, and Baker's Island, the steamer was overtaken by a "fearful squall" on July 4, 1898. Although there was less than 7 feet of water, eight women and children were lost. (Courtesy Cressy Collection.)

The Woodbury Shoe Company, Now 50 Rantoul Street (c. 1912 Postcard). Small, one-room ten-footers, which dotted most New England towns in the 19th century, were located near the home of the shoemaker, or "cordwainer." In these small buildings, cordwainers made shoes for their families and for barter or sale. When shoe manufacturing became more of a growing and competitive business around the 1850s, wooden factories, and then larger brick ones, were built to fill production demands. The Woodbury Shoe Company was one of the largest brick shoe factories in the city, with two stair towers for access to the upper floors. When the company was incorporated in 1902 with capital of $100,000, Hezekiah O. Woodbury was the president, William T. Varina was the vice president, Orpheus L. Woodbury was the secretary, and Rufus H. Woodbury was the treasurer. (Courtesy Beverly Public Library.)

A Sewing Room in the Woodbury Shoe Company, 50 Rantoul Street (c. 1910 Photograph). In 1837, when the shoemaking industry was in its infancy, there were about 300 men and 200 women employed in the manufacture of footwear. The value of boots and shoes turned out that year was $60,000, and the population of the town was 4,609. By 1890, one-third of all Beverly men and one-third of employable women found work in the shoe factories around Rantoul Street. (Courtesy Ralph A. Parisella.)

THE CUSHING CARRIAGE MANUFACTORY, CORNER OF RANTOUL AND PLEASANT STREETS (C. 1870 PHOTOGRAPH). Taking a break on a sunny summer's day, employees of the John T. Cushing Jr. carriage factory pose in front of the mid-19th-century building before resuming work on the four assorted vehicles. (Courtesy Finch and Rose Collection.)

THE BEVERLY POST OFFICE, 151 RANTOUL STREET (C. 1912 POSTCARD). Classical architectural symmetry defines the "new" post office, which was constructed of limestone in 1910, when William Howard Taft was president of the United States. At the time, His Excellency Eben S. Draper was governor of the Commonwealth of Massachusetts, and His Honor Charles H. Trowt was mayor of Beverly. Patrons of the past, and those of today, may still use the side entrance on Broadway.

A GATHERING OF SOME DISTINGUISHED CITIZENS AND POSTAL EMPLOYEES, 151 RANTOUL STREET (1923 PHOTOGRAPH). In 1923, Joseph E. Herrick was the city's postmaster, Calvin P. Pierce was the assistant postmaster, and Charles A. Larcom (standing in the first row, far right) was the superintendent. (Courtesy Clayton Collection.)

Kransberg's, 356 Rantoul Street (1928 Photograph). Large of hand and heart (as his grandson remembers him), Philip Kransberg, who was listed as a "junk" dealer in the 1922 city directory, arranges a phonograph on a Victorian occasional table in the family's first furniture store. (Courtesy Edward L. Kransberg.)

Kransberg's, 363 Rantoul Street (c. 1935 Photograph). The Kransberg family purchased this building in 1934 from the Beverly Mattress Company. They added an extension in 1945, moved to 301 Cabot Street in 1957, and closed the business in 1988. In 1952, Samuel G. Kransberg was the president and manager, Philip was the treasurer, John N. was the assistant treasurer, Harry L. was a clerk, and Edward L. was a salesman. During the firm's heyday, it offered quality furniture such as Colonial Creations, Georgetown Galleries Solid Mahogany, as well as Bengal Ranges and Daystrom Chrome Furniture. In the late 19th century, W.C. Packard operated a furniture and carpet store at 116 Cabot Street that specialized in rattan and summer furniture as well as "straw mattings [for floors] in great variety." (Courtesy Kransberg Collection.)

THE PHILIP KRANSBERG FAMILY (C. 1905 PHOTOGRAPH). Philip and Esther Kransberg, who were born in Minsk, Russia, pose with their children, Pearl and Samuel, in a local photographer's studio to document their new lives together. Many Beverlyites of the Jewish faith worshiped at the Sons of Abraham and Isaac Synagogue, which was located at 37 Bow Street around this time. Ten years after it was organized in 1905, the rabbi was Charles Gindea. The Beverly Jewish Lodge, No. 458, met at the synagogue, and the Independent Order of United Hebrews, Essex County Lodge, No. 59, met at 124 Cabot Street. (Courtesy Kransberg Collection.)

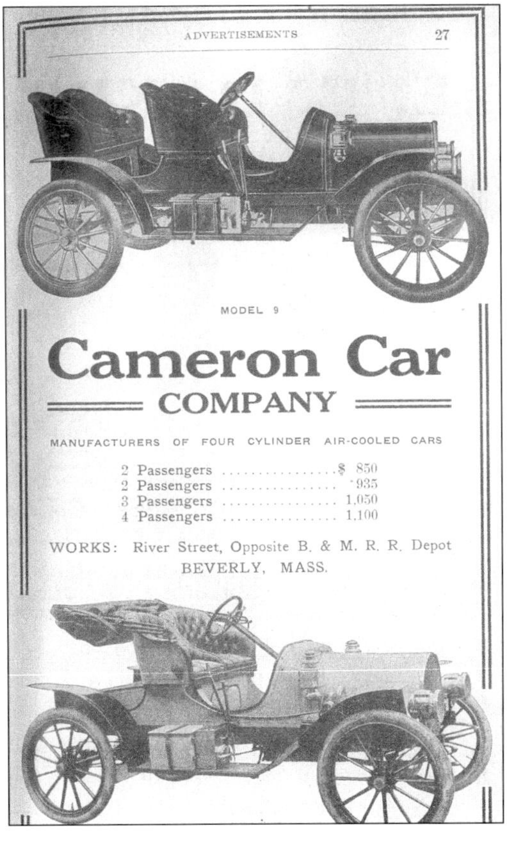

A CAMERON CAR ADVERTISEMENT (1909). Between 1886 and 1918, seven automobile manufacturers were located in the Garden City, producing vehicles such as the Philbrick Steamer (1886), the Cameron Car (1908–1912), and "the Beverly Wagon" (1905–1907), a local name for an early family station wagon. The Cameron Car Company, with sales headquarters in New York City, was located on River Street behind the train station in the former Upton Auto & Truck Company. Four-cylinder, air-cooled cars (runabouts, roadsters, and touring cars) retailed between $900 and $1,110, and the same six-cylinder models were priced at $1,500. (Courtesy Beverly Public Library.)

BEVERLY HIGH SCHOOL, 7 SOHIER ROAD (C. 1930 POSTCARD). To remind students and older citizens of their patriotism, an American flag flew over the city's modern high school, built in 1923 of brick and cast concrete with interesting architectural details. (Courtesy Atherton Collection.)

STUDENTS SELLING WAR STAMPS AND BONDS (1945 PHOTOGRAPH). Defense-minded students gathered in room 201 in the high school every Tuesday morning to take orders for war stamps and bonds. They kept records, counted and rolled the money, made up the stamp order, and took the money to a bank, where they collected the stamps and bonds. Shown, from left to right, are the following: (sitting) Christine Campbell, Miss Watters (adviser), Eleanor Ricci, and Shirley Reinhold; (standing) John Gobeille, Myrtle Raymond, Malissa Thomas, and John Truesdale. (Courtesy Kransberg Collection.)

THORNDIKE STREET LOOKING EAST FROM ENDICOTT STREET (C. 1900 POSTCARD). At least four Thorndikes built homes on Hale Street in Beverly Cove during a 30-year period in the 18th century. John Thorndike Jr. erected his home at No. 182 in 1723–1727. Andrew Thorndike built his dwelling at No. 193 in 1754. The cordwainer James Thorndike's house at No. 232 was raised in 1723. Peter Thorndike, a mariner, crossed the finished threshold of his new home at No. 238 in 1723. (Courtesy Beverly Public Library.)

WASHINGTON STREET NEAR THE CORNER OF CABOT STREET (C. 1900 POSTCARD). With the death of the former first president of the United States in December 1799, an outpouring of national grief resulted in the naming of children, streets, or organizations for the "father of his country." Washington Street was laid out in 1803. No. 12 (left) was built in 1832 and was the home of Capt. Ezra Foster, a master mariner in the China Trade. The classic Greek Revival temple (right, behind the trees) has three large columns and was erected in 1838 for silversmith Oliver Trask.

WATER STREET ALONG THE HARBOR (C. 1895 POSTCARD). The 1872 Beverly map (see p. 13) states at the beginning of the subscribers' business directory that it is "a beautiful and growing town [it became a city in 1894], and one of its many advantages is its large and safe harbour, whose waters are deep enough for the navigation of the largest vessels." As late as 1909, there were 11 active wharves in the city. Most of them were off Water Street: the Sprague, Breed & Brown Wharf (No. 7), the Salem Water Works Wharf (No. 47), Central Wharf (No. 50), Girdler's Wharf (No. 71–81), Gulf Refining Company Wharf (No. 85–115), and the Pickett Coal Company Wharf (No. 150).

FISHING OFF THE WHARF (C. 1900 POSTCARD). Beverly and Marblehead were both well-known fishing ports in the 18th century. In 1785, the period between the Revolutionary War and the War of 1812, there were 30 schooners fishing from Beverly's port. The industry was localized in the summer, but during the winter trade was carried on with southern ports, the West Indies, and the Cape Verde Islands. By 1790, it was the only town that had increased its catch and tonnage over pre-Revolutionary figures. A scant five years later, the tonnage had increased even more. Before he became president of Yale College in 1795, Timothy Dwight traveled through New England and wrote that Beverly fishermen were "distinguished for good order, industry, sober manners, and sound morals" unlike their Marblehead counterparts.

COAL BUSINESSES ALONG THE HARBOR (C. 1900 POSTCARD). The firm of Sprague, Breed & Brown advertised that it had plenty of coal for sale at the lowest market prices in 1900. Varieties offered included "Scranton Stove, Chestnut, Egg, Broken, Franklin, and Shamokin Stove." One of their competitors, the Salem and Beverly Coal Company (located at Steamboat Wharf in Beverly) sold "Nova Scotia wood, cannel coal, and yellow birch [for open fires]" as well as "Shamokin and Lykens Valley coal." Although the company's wharf was only 15 feet at low tide, vessels such as "steam yachts [could be] cooled promptly."

THE JUBILEE YACHT CLUB, TUCK'S POINT (C. 1900 POSTCARD). Organized in November 1893 and incorporated three years later, the Jubilee Yacht Club is prominently situated at the entrance to the inner harbor. In 1915, club meetings were held on the second Tuesday of each month, with officers being elected annually in January. Tuck's Point was named during the first decade of the 18th century. In the last decade of the 19th century, the Okahahwis Canoe Club (organized in 1899) was located near the yacht club.

CAPT. HUGH HILL'S SHIP CHANDLERY, 62 WATER STREET (C. 1977 PHOTOGRAPH). A ship chandler sold all the necessary objects that a mariner or fisherman needed to pursue his business. Owned by Captain Hill, this late-18th-century brick building (the three-story section) has been altered by later owners. Businesses similar to this one have changed the maritime atmosphere of Water Street. Around 1900, several fish flake yards had been set up along the waterfront; one such odoriferous yard was owned by David Crowell at 107 Water Street. (Courtesy Finch and Rose Collection.)

THE *LETTIE G. HOWARD* SAILING OFF THE MAINE COAST. Built in Essex, Massachusetts, in 1893, this 75-foot fishing schooner (known as a "Georgesman" for the Georges Bank area where it fished) is the only surviving one of its type. Ordered by a Beverly fisherman and named for his daughter, the *Lettie G. Howard* was purchased by the South Street Seaport Museum in New York City in 1968 and was subsequently restored. (Courtesy Erik A.R. Ronnberg Jr.)

Three

"The Shoe"

An Aerial View of the United Shoe Machinery Corporation, Elliott Street (Mid-20th-Century Photograph). The centrally located smokestack of the Shoe, with its prominent lettering, identifies the rectangular compound of Beverly's largest single business, which was in operation between 1905 and 1987. Designed by construction engineer Ernest L. Ransome, whose reinforced concrete company was located at 11 Broadway in New York, the main buildings that comprise the corporation were the largest of their kind in the world before 1940. The USM was also the largest employer of the city's workforce, and jobs there were much sought after. As many as 5,000 people punched time clocks at the Shoe during World War I, in an ideal working environment. It featured acres of daylight-flooded windows, a mechanical ventilation system, large and clean restrooms, an in-house medical facility, an on-site vocational school for prospective workers, and a clubhouse with a ballroom. Good wages and benevolent working conditions kept the employees loyal and happy, accident-free, and not in any need to unionize. The USM had a virtual monopoly on shoe machinery sold and serviced for decades, but its dominance in the industry brought about the company's demise. Sixty years after an antitrust suit was directed against it in 1911, the company was broken up and eventually moved to Wilmington, Massachusetts. New life was breathed into the historic structures on the 80-acre site in May 1996, when Cummings Properties of Woburn, Massachusetts, began a sensitive renovation and modern marketing plan. (Courtesy Cummings Properties.)

WORK IN PROGRESS (AUGUST 1, 1904 PHOTOGRAPH). Most of the construction workers posing for this unusual picture were brought from Italy. Many stayed and were absorbed into Beverly's growing melting pot. (Courtesy Cummings Properties.)

LEDGES VS. CONCRETE (C. 1904 PHOTOGRAPH). Blasting of dense ledges on the site was time-consuming and difficult work for those entrusted with that job. The pitched-roof foundry and the main building with its flat roof have taken shape against what was then a rural background. On September 21, 1904, it was reported that one construction worker was killed and several others were badly injured when a ladder collapsed. (Courtesy Cummings Properties.)

THE FINISHED FACTORY (C. 1920S POSTCARD). With the completion of construction on the site and the opening of the large facility, nonlocal employees used this Boston and Maine Railroad stop to travel to work. Three-decker houses on Simon, Grant, Mill, and Ropes Streets were built for local factory workers so they could walk to work. Individual houses built on and off Mckay Street, the other side of the Shoe, provided residences for upper-echelon employees.

A Typical Machinery Production Area (c. 1930s Photograph). Large windows allow bright light to fill the factory's work spaces, always swept clean by the night crew. The on-site powerhouse, located in a separate building to the left of the complex, was used to generate steam that was fed through underground tunnels for operating a series of flywheels, pulleys, and long leather belts. Soon, this area will be filled with the noise of machines and men. (Courtesy Cummings Properties.)

SECURING A SOLE (C. 1927 PHOTOGRAPH). A native of Danvers, Dennis James Sullivan was born during America's centennial year. He is shown here in a professional photograph with a painted backdrop. He and his son, Frank, were designated as "roadmen." The two were repairmen who often traveled together to many states to fix lasting machines and to train other men for the job. Jan Matzeliger, a Dutch Guinan of African descent, invented and patented the first lasting machine in 1883. (Courtesy Alice J. Sullivan.)

SEWING AN UPPER (C. 1950 PHOTOGRAPH). Born in Lynn in 1901, Frank Andrew Sullivan demonstrates the ease of operation with which this model of a lasting machine works. He and his father, Dennis, were known as the "Sullivan brothers," as they appeared to be about the same age—with his premature white hair, the son looked almost as old as his father! (Courtesy Sullivan Collection.)

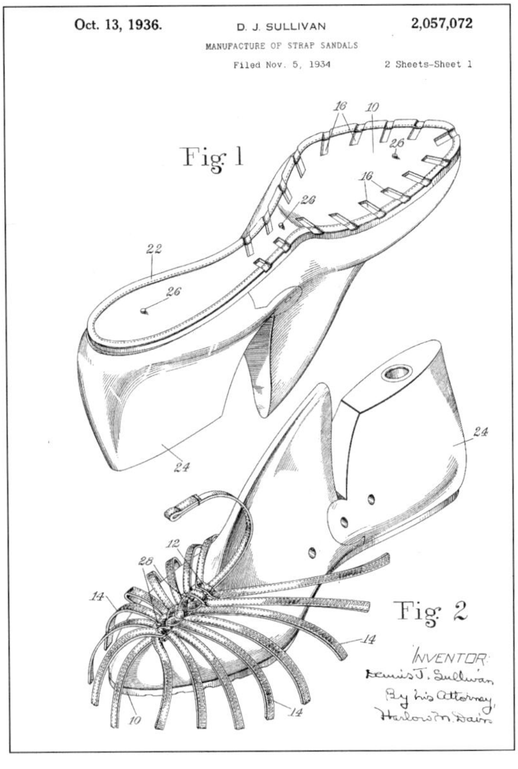

AN UNUSUAL MUSICAL GROUP (C. 1906 PHOTOGRAPH). Dressed in formal or funny attire, these gentlemen pose in front of a good-sized tent for an early event sponsored by the USM. (Courtesy Cummings Properties.)

A SAMPLE PATENT (OCTOBER 13, 1936). Showing one of several inventions patented by Dennis J. Sullivan, this illustration relates to "improvements in the manufacture of strap sandals and other shoes of the type wherein the shoe is adapted to be retained in place upon the foot by means of straps or the like which extend upwardly from the lateral edge portions of the sole. [This] improved method renders unnecessary the initial insertion and subsequent withdrawal of tacks or other temporary fastening devices for holding the straps in overlasted relation to the insole." (Courtesy Sullivan Collection.)

THE USM CLUBHOUSE, 134 MCKAY STREET (C. 1920S POSTCARD). Gables both large and small provide light to the third-floor rooms of the wood and stucco Scottish Tudor–style structure, which was built in 1910 as a recreational facility for employees. Tennis courts and landscaped grounds added to the club's appeal and charm. The United Shoe Machinery Athletic Association was organized that same year and held its annual meeting the first Tuesday in September at the clubhouse.

EXAMINING A TROPHY (C. 1910 PHOTOGRAPH). Six Edwardian gentlemen, all wearing starched collars and high-laced leather shoes, discuss the merits of this sterling silver trophy placed on a processed cowhide. (Courtesy Cummings Properties.)

A GATHERING OF THE QUARTER CENTURY CLUB ON THE GROUNDS OF THE CLUBHOUSE (C. 1970S PHOTOGRAPH). Former executives of the USM greet one another and exchange past and present stories, as do their wives or special guests. The first annual meeting of the Quarter Century Club was held on June 25, 1927, as by that time there were many 25-year employees, and the membership continued to grow. The gentleman wearing black glasses (lower right, talking to the woman) is William Houghton of Marblehead. When Houghton retired from the Shoe, he volunteered for many years as a museum carpenter at the former Essex Institute in Salem.

Four

Lynch Park and Some Other Gardens

The Italian Gardens, David S. Lynch Memorial Park, 55 Ober Street (c. 1945 Postcard). Located on Burgess Point in Beverly Cove, this classically inspired garden is near the fort that protected Beverly during the Revolutionary War period. The mansion house where President Taft and his family summered for three years was situated on the grounds until the irate owner, Mrs. Robert Dawson Evans, decided to replace it with a sunken garden. In 1943, upon the death of Miss Hunt, the last spinster sister of the late Mrs. Evans, the estate (which had been left to the Beverly Hospital) was acquired by the city and opened that summer as a memorial to the munificent gentleman. A booklet on Beverly parks notes, "The various sections of the [David S. Lynch Memorial] park have fitted into our community life in many ways and are places of beauty at all seasons and at all hours of the day."

THE ENTRANCE TO THE DAWSON HALL TEA ROOM, DAVID S. LYNCH MEMORIAL PARK (C. 1945 POSTCARD). Dawson Hall, a picturesque mansion house, was built in the seaside park by Benjamin Burgess of Boston, for whom Burgess Point was named. The 15 acres of land where it stood included a courtyard, stable, monastery, beach, and fragrant rose garden. Socially prominent ladies and gentlemen (and others with blood not so blue) enjoyed sipping a cup of afternoon tea in the pleasant setting.

THE ROSE GARDEN, DAVID S. LYNCH MEMORIAL PARK (C. 1945 POSTCARD). Patterned brick walkways lead visitors around the perimeter of the partially walled garden and downstairs into the sunken area, where polychrome roses perfume the summer air. A pair of recumbent marble lions scan the parterre, which features a pavilion with ten stop-fluted Doric columns and a slate roof (previous page). An antique marble settee with carved winged caryatid armrests invites contemplation.

"A RIOT OF COLOR," DAVID S. LYNCH MEMORIAL PARK (C. 1945 POSTCARD). The stately arched colonnade that faced the beach was toppled during a hurricane in the 1950s. A bronze plaque on the brick wall behind it states that the Beverly Improvement Society has contributed annually to the beautification of the garden since it was opened to the public in 1943. Although not as extravagantly planted, or as pristine as in the past, the garden is a colorful oasis of roses and annual flowers in a lovely seaside surrounding.

THE FALCONER AND A LADY FRIEND, DAVID S. LYNCH MEMORIAL PARK (C. 1945 PHOTOGRAPH). While touring Essex County, fun-loving Helen Kristofferson, a secretary in the Wall Street district, was attracted to the statue of a Renaissance falconer and posed for this snapshot taken by her Beverly friend, Rita St. Pierre. The Gorham Manufacturing Company of Providence, Rhode Island, cast the bronze statue whose back is to the adjacent beach. (Courtesy St. Pierre Collection.)

The Spaulding Garden, Paine Avenue, Pride's Crossing (c. 1910 Postcard). The extensive garden that William S. and John T. Spaulding enjoyed required the help of many employees both in and out of the several greenhouses. Benjamin Larcom was a florist who maintained greenhouses on Essex Street at the corner of Jackson Street in the late 1880s. He specialized in flowering and ornamental plants. He also made bouquets and sold loose flowers and sheaves of wheat. The funeral and table designs he arranged were made to order, then as now. (Courtesy Beverly Public Library.)

The Dudley L. Pickman Gardens, 188 Hale Street (Early-20th-Century Postcard). Manicured shrubs, unusual flowers, a gravel walkway, and a densely planted backdrop make these gardens look special and inviting. Dudley L. Pickman owned and operated the North Shore Ferneries Company, of which he was the president, and his namesake was the treasurer. (Courtesy Beverly Public Library.)

Five

The Summer White House

President Taft and His Summer Home on Burgess Point (1910 Postcard). During the first months of his only term as the 27th U.S. president, portly William Howard Taft (1857–1930) made plans for his family's vacation, opting to use the presidential yacht USS *Mayflower*. The yacht had been used in 1907 by his predecessor and mentor, Teddy Roosevelt, to attend the laying of the cornerstone of the Pilgrim Monument in Provincetown. After close friends had suggested Beverly as a suitable spot for Taft and his family, he leased the Robert Dawson Evans estate on Burgess Point on April 12, 1909. The commodious 14-room, Shingle-style "cottage" was ideal the first three summers, but before the last vacation of his presidency, Taft, who had grown fond of the area and who enjoyed new friendships made there, was forced to find a new summer dwelling—Parramatta in the Montserrat section of the Garden City.

THE ENTRANCE TO PRESIDENT TAFT'S SUMMER HOME, OFF OBER STREET (C. 1910 POSTCARD). A curved stone fence and gateposts identify the entrance to the summer White House in the city's Cove section. The other entrance to Lynch Park is opposite the 1734 house, built by mariner Hugh Woodberry.

THE SUMMER WHITE HOUSE (C. 1910 POSTCARD). Built for A.B. Turner, the picturesque dwelling was later owned by Mr. and Mrs. Robert Dawson Evans, whose money enabled the Museum of Fine Arts, Boston, to construct the rear entrance to that magnificent institution. Upon realizing that souvenir hunters were actually destroying parts of the house and trampling the garden, the widow Evans made a bold move by having the house removed from its foundation and then transported by barge to Peach's Point in Marblehead. The Italian garden was then designed to fill the space and blot out the owner's unhappy memory of the presidential summer lease.

The First Family (c. 1910 Postcard). Dressed in their Edwardian finery, President Taft, his wife, Helen ("Nellie"), and their children—Helen (a Bryn Mawr student), Charlie, and Robert (a recent Yale graduate)—pose before motoring to a Sunday morning service at the First Parish Unitarian church. (Courtesy Clayton Collection.)

The Garage on the Evans Estate (c. 1910 Postcard). A sizable stable, or garage, for the period, this Shingle-style behemoth was where the spit-and-polish vehicle was stored. The Taft family used this vehicle on their many exploratory jaunts around Essex County, long before serious thought was given to presidential protection. Taft was the third president to travel in an automobile.

PARRAMATTA, 70 CORNING STREET (C. 1915 POSTCARD). Perched on a ledge in Montserrat (nicknamed "monster rat" by many locals), the 18-room mansion was the estate of the late Henry W. Peabody, who had named it for the countryside around Parramatta, Australia. For one brief summer, the Taft family enjoyed the Japanese garden, the artificial pond, the tennis courts, and especially the nine-hole golf course, the president's favorite. (Courtesy Clayton Collection.)

THE PRESIDENTIAL YACHT USS *MAYFLOWER* IN BEVERLY HARBOR (C. 1910 POSTCARD). The Taft family first arrived off Burgess Point on the patriotic day of July 4, 1909. A sleek white-painted steam yacht, the *Mayflower* was aptly named for its second visit to the tip of Cape Cod when President Taft dedicated the Pilgrim Monument on August 5, 1910. In an interview conducted there, the jovial chief executive mentioned, "[The yacht] is somewhat different in size and comfort and in luxury from that which brought the Pilgrims, but there are certain stories I should like to deny. We have no special bath tubs made for any executive of any particular size (laughter). I don't know whether they had bath tubs on the *Mayflower*. Presumably it was pretty cold for a bath when they arrived in these waters."

Six

RYAL SIDE

A RYAL SIDE SCENE (EARLY-20TH-CENTURY POSTCARD). The section of Beverly known as Ryal, or Rial Side, was named for William Royall, a cooper (barrel maker) who arrived in the area in 1629. Ryal Side begins at the Bass River (which flows from the Danvers River) and includes peripheral streets emanating from Bridge Street (beginning at the bridge) and stretches to the Danvers line. Built in 1907, the smaller of the two bridges many Beverlyites cross each day is on Kernwood Street and is called the Danvers River Bridge or Kernwood Bridge.

OBEAR PARK LOOKING EAST TO THE BOSTON AND MAINE RAILROAD BRIDGE (EARLY-20TH-CENTURY POSTCARD). A many-gabled cottage with a wraparound piazza sits prominently along the Danvers River near the promontory designated as Obear Park on July 5, 1937. The park, which is situated at the end of Livingstone Avenue, "was secured by the City of Beverly through the efforts of Capt. Benjamin L. Ober." It was dedicated by the Honorable Daniel E. McLean, who was the mayor that year. (Courtesy Beverly Public Library.)

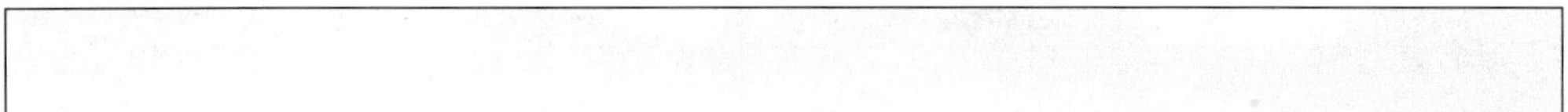

BATES PARK (C. 1905 POSTCARD). The waterfront area known as Bates Park is a neighborhood of small cottages also along the Danvers River. The park has vistas of the marina in Danversport, the sweeping lawn of the Kernwood Country Club in Salem (founded in 1914), and the new Veterans' Memorial Bridge that connects Beverly to Salem.

A NONEXPLOSIVE CHOO-CHOO TRAIN, 7 GREGG STREET (C. 1937 PHOTOGRAPH). Young engineer Paul Larcom poses in the backyard of the family home with two passengers, Barbara Todd and Hugh Moran, on the toy train his father, Sidney, made out of empty explosives boxes. (Courtesy Larcom Collection.)

A RYAL SIDE PARADE (C. 1977 PHOTOGRAPH). An unidentified clown with bright red hair and a winning smile amuses onlookers in the annual parade, which has been sponsored by the Ryal Side Civic Association since the 1950s. The family-oriented parade begins at the corner of Bridge Street and Western Avenue and ends about 2 miles later at Obear Park, where a carnival, free ice cream and games, and fireworks delight old and young. (Courtesy private collection.)

A Business Transaction at Ralph's Market, 81 Bridge Street (c. 1963 Photograph). A lovely trapeze artist holding a bottle of Coca-Cola smiles down on the assorted grocery store merchandise that young Ralph Parisella has displayed on the shelves and counter in the neighborhood market he opened in 1955. (Courtesy Parisella Collection.)

A Local "Blue Law" Cartoon (1968 Drawing by Walt Fournier). Ralph Parisella, the president and treasurer of the market that bears his name, brought suit against the City of Beverly, Mayor Carl V. Joslin, and police officials in February 1968 when he was notified by the police that he would be brought into court if he opened his store on Sundays. Attorney Bertram Glovsky's argument for his client persuaded jurors of the Massachusetts Supreme Judicial Court to let Parisella and other retailers with more than two employees remain open to sell such basics as newspapers, bakery and tobacco products, baby foods, fresh fruit and vegetables, sanitary supplies, and similar items. (Courtesy the *Salem Evening News*.)

Seven

NORTH BEVERLY

FOSTER'S CORNER, THE INTERSECTION OF CABOT, DODGE, AND MCKAY STREETS (C. 1930 PHOTOGRAPH). The once rural area of North Beverly begins at the corner of Cabot and Balch Streets, where the John Balch House is located, and proceeds slightly left through Foster's Corner and beyond the Beverly Municipal Airport to the Wenham town line. Dodge Street starts to the right of the fire station, crosses the railroad tracks where the former wood-framed North Beverly train station was situated and ends at the Wenham town line. Dodge Street also flows into Enon Street (to the left of the train tracks), ending at another Wenham town line. The long, wood-framed building was a branch of the First National Store before Henry Swanson acquired the property in 1941, had it razed, and then built the first Henry's Market on the site. (Courtesy Henry's of North Beverly.)

THE WINSLOW SCHOOL, CORNER OF MCKAY AND BALCH STREETS (EARLY-20TH-CENTURY POSTCARD). The town's first grammar school was established in 1700, and the Winslow School was built 210 years later near the head of the "Shoe Pond." The school lost its unique appearance with the removal of the Flemish gables. A 1930 Massachusetts Bay Colony tercentenary sign by the pond refers to the "Planters Path to Their Landing Place."

THE WINSLOW ESTATES, 545 AND 555 CABOT STREET (C. 1913 POSTCARD). Now on the grounds of the Shore Country Day School, the Colonial Revival Sidney W. Winslow House (right) at 545 Cabot Street was built for the founder and first president of the United Shoe Machinery Corporation. The Shingle-style Herbert F. Winslow House (since demolished) was built for his real estate son. Sidney Winslow was also the treasurer of the Beverly Gas and Electric Company; he maintained an office at 36 Cabot Street. The blue and white porcelain automobile license plate, No. 1817 (now in a private collection), was a feature on his 1909 Renault. (Courtesy Beverly Public Library.)

Horace Foster's Grocery Store, 588 Cabot Street (c. 1905 Photograph). As an enterprising merchant, Horace Foster sold hay and grain, wood and coal, and had a laundry office in the substantial structure with its attached stable. Galvanized milk containers, flats of flowers, and assorted bottles are on the stair landing by the two gents. Two horseless vehicles sit idly by inside the white picket fence, and painting supplies are advertised on the rails of the property gate. Horace "Hoddie" and Eliza A. Foster resided at 590 Dodge Street. (Courtesy Henry's Market Collection.)

Henry's Super Market, Cooch's Barber Shop, and the John Hyde Pharmacy, Foster's Corner (c. 1956 Photograph). A popular landmark for many years, the L-shaped building was remodeled with the loss of Cooch's Barber Shop and the John Hyde Pharmacy to make room for the expansion of the market. (Courtesy Henry's Market Collection.)

THE NORTH BEVERLY FIRE STATION, 2 DODGE STREET (C. 1940S PHOTOGRAPH). Built in the early 20th century, the fire station is a visible landmark as one approaches it along Cabot Street. A team of horses was kept in the building before the apparatus became mechanized. (Courtesy Atherton Collection.)

PRELIMINARY CONSTRUCTION OF THE CABOT STREET OVERPASS (C. 1945 PHOTOGRAPH). Several nurseries, such as the one run by the Southworth Brothers, were located in the surrounding area that became part of busy Route 128 when it was completed in the early 1950s. The steel and concrete bridge abutments were faced with granite, as were those at the Dodge Street Overpass, which was erected thereafter. (Courtesy Atherton Collection.)

AN ARCHITECTURAL CONVERSION, THE SECOND CONGREGATIONAL CHURCH, CORNER OF CABOT AND CONANT STREETS (C. 1955 PHOTOGRAPH). Raised in 1714 as a meetinghouse, Beverly's Upper Parish church was remodeled in the Greek Revival style *c.* 1853. It was restored in the Colonial style c. 1929 and was renovated in 1955–1956 by rotating it 90 degrees and adding it to the new structure at the right. The Reverend John Chipman, M.A., (1690–1775) was the first minister, and the slate gravestone featuring his portrait effigy has a lengthy Latin inscription on it. Located behind the church along Route 97 is the North Beverly Cemetery. (Courtesy Atherton Collection.)

HOOD'S CHERRY HILL FARM, 131 CONANT STREET (C. 1940S POSTCARD). One of the oldest operating farms in America, Cherry Hill Farm was acquired by H.P. Hood and Sons in 1912 and was run much like a "gentleman's farm." A spotless environment with about 500 contented cows on special bovine diets appealed to young families and groups of schoolchildren until the farm closed in 1965. The picnic area, petting zoo, and the ice-cream stand were special attractions remembered by the farm's many visitors. (Courtesy Clayton Collection.)

A FOR LEASE ADVERTISEMENT, BEVERLY MUNICIPAL AIRPORT, L.P. HENDERSON ROAD OFF CABOT STREET (C. 1955). Built in 1928 through the cooperation of the Beverly Aero Club and the chamber of commerce (and later taken over by the city), this transportation resource is located about 20 miles from Boston's Logan International Airport. The U.S. Navy operated the airport under a joint agreement with the city during World War II. In 1950, it was formally returned to Beverly. (Courtesy Beverly Municipal Airport.)

A GROUP OF YOUNG AVIATORS, BEVERLY AIRPORT (C. 1938 PHOTOGRAPH). Posing in front of Harold Morganstern's Stinson SM-8A monoplane are, from left to right, George Foster, Alice Jackson, Steve Cook, ? Morganstern, and an unidentified friend. (Courtesy Larcom Collection.)

AN AIRSHOW AT THE BEVERLY AIRPORT (1968 PHOTOGRAPH). The John Mountan Field was filled with sparkling clean airplanes and enthusiastic visitors for the summer airshow. During an air meet in the 1940s, Piper cubs, Taylor cubs, Luscombs, Stinsons, and other small planes were flown by local aviators and by pilots from other airports. (Courtesy Beverly Municipal Airport.)

A CAPTIVATED AUDIENCE AT THE AIRSHOW (1968 PHOTOGRAPH). Mesmerized youngsters, many fantasizing about being in the cockpit, watch as one or two pilots maneuver their planes overhead. (Courtesy Beverly Municipal Airport.)

THE BEVERLY COTTON MILL, 4 DODGE STREET (REPRODUCTION OF 1897 WASH DRAWING BY GEORGE ELMER BROWNE). The country's first cotton mill (established in 1787 to the right of the fire station) was visited by George Washington on October 30, 1789, while he was on his New England tour. The illustrious leader noted that "the Cotton Manufactory, which seems to be carrying on with spirit by the Cabbots [*sic*] . . . the whole seemed perfect and the cotton stuffs which they turn out, excellent of their kind; warp and filling both are now of Coton [*sic*]." A slate marker to the far right of the fire station commemorates the history of the business venture, which was in operation until 1815. The wooden building was destroyed by fire in 1828. (Courtesy private collection.)

CONSTRUCTION OF SLAB HOUSES ON LONGMEADOW ROAD (C. 1950S PHOTOGRAPH). These post–World War II simple structures without cellars were similar to the concrete slab houses built around this time by the Campanelli Corporation on the former Raymond Farm. Eager first-time house buyers purchased them for $18,000 each. (Courtesy Atherton Collection.)

A NORTH BEVERLY BONFIRE STACK IN THE LONGMEADOW ROAD AREA (JULY 4, 1940). Monster bonfires that illuminated the sky the night before the Fourth of July were an awe-inspiring spectacle attended by as many as 10,000 people. Begun by local firefighters and neighbors in 1935 with a stocky pile of old barrels, tires, and hay, the more traditional bonfire stack of grease-soaked barrels grew each year (106 feet in 1940) until the late 1950s, when the community's summer social event was curtailed. (Courtesy Atherton Collection.)

LAWRENCE ATHERTON'S SERVICE STATION, 1 AND 3 DODGE STREET (C. 1950S PHOTOGRAPH). "Shellubrication" was a fancy word for a special service provided by this local gas station. Murphy's Garage, located to the right of this two-business structure, serviced and sold vehicles. (Courtesy Atherton Collection.)

"CLAMMING IT UP" NEAR THE DODGE STREET OVERPASS (C. 1953 PHOTOGRAPH). These Beverlyites, just returning from the Essex River clam flats, pose with their containers of bivalve mollusks. From left to right are Bob Atherton (wearing his high school hockey shirt), his good-humored father, Larry (owner of the Atherton service station), and Neal Mitchell, an employee of the Almy, Bigelow & Washburn department store. (Courtesy Atherton Collection.)

CHINALAND RESTAURANT, 48 DODGE STREET (C. 1956 PHOTOGRAPH). In 1952, Frank Chin was the vice president of the first oriental eatery on the site, and Peter Leong was the manager. On October 14, 1903, a Chinese person who resided in Beverly became the first registered Asian voter in Essex County. (Courtesy Atherton Collection.)

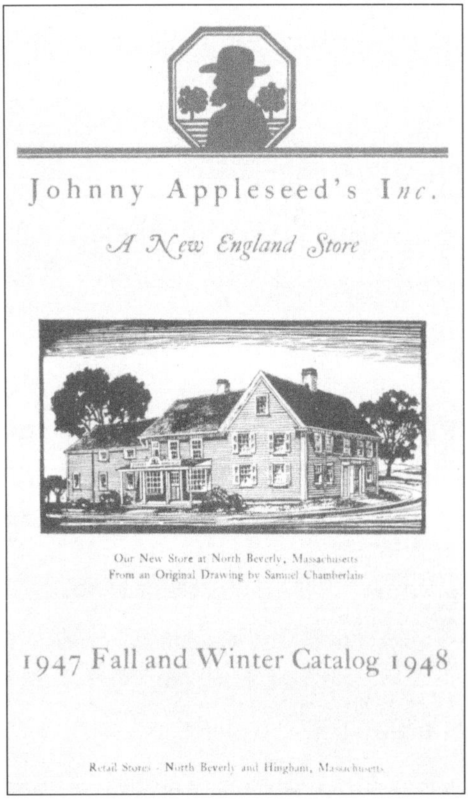

A JOHNNY APPLESEED'S CATALOG (1947–1948). Marblehead artist and gourmand Samuel Chamberlain (1895–1975) made this pen-and-ink drawing of the firm's premier location at 50 Dodge Street for founder Samuel Batchelder. Some of the winter apparel for skiing listed and illustrated in the catalog includes wool head bands for $1.00, "boy's gabardine ski trousers that really wear!" for $9.75, rugged woolen ragg socks for $1.00, and men's ski mittens with soft buckskin palms for $4.25. (Courtesy Appleseeds.)

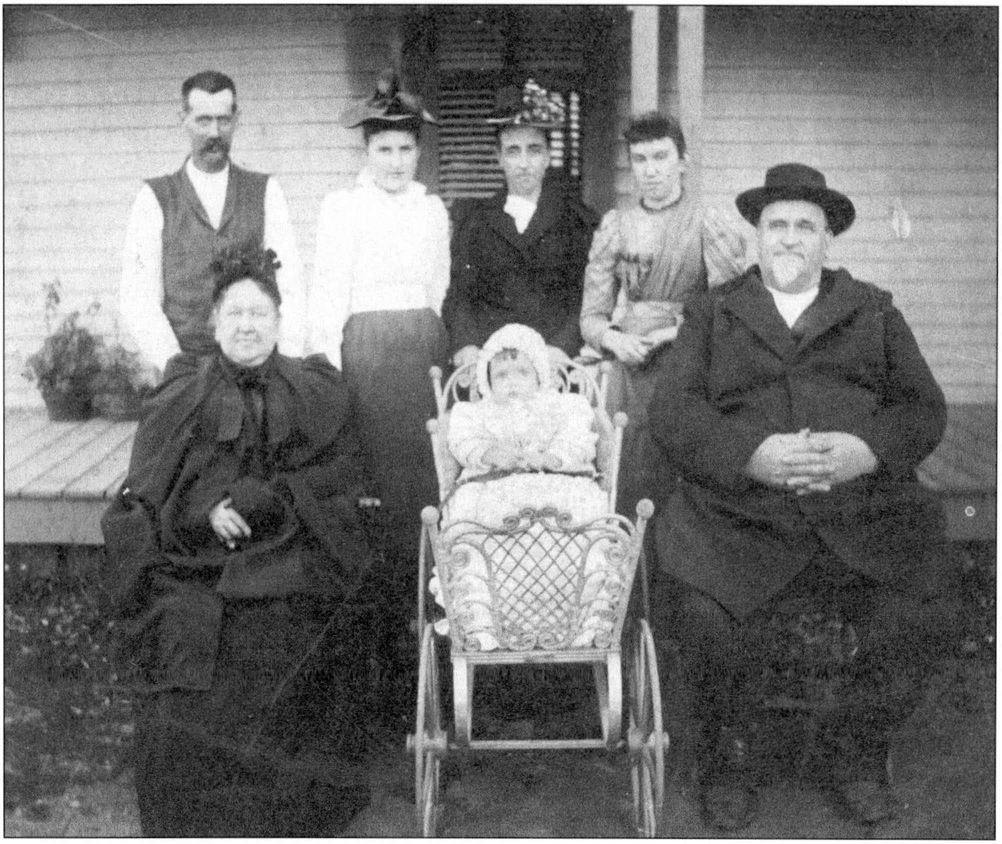

WOODBURY AND ANDREWS FAMILY MEMBERS ON THE EAST PORCH OF THE PETER WOODBURY HOUSE, 82 DODGE STREET (1902 PHOTOGRAPH). Elderly Mary and Peter Woodbury flank baby Mabel Woodbury Andrews, the only child of Joseph F. Andrews and Lucy Storey Andrews. This portrait was taken to document the two families and the transition of ownership of the home that had been in the Woodbury family since it was built, *c*. 1691. In the back row are, from left to right, Joseph F. Andrews, Olive Andrews (Joseph's sister), Lucy Storey Andrews, and "hired girl" Flora Claflin. (Courtesy Cressy Collection.)

A COLLECTION OF NATIVE AMERICAN ARTIFACTS (EARLY-20TH-CENTURY PHOTOGRAPH). This outstanding assortment of stone, dating back thousands of years, consists of agricultural tools, and hunting and fishing implements. They were unearthed in the fields behind the Peter Woodbury House by Joseph F. Andrews around the turn of the century. The large and heavily grooved axehead in the middle row, far left, is 8 inches long. An unusually large fishing line weight is in the top row, fourth from the right. (Courtesy Cressy Collection.)

The Peter Woodbury House, 82 Dodge Street (c. 1935 Photograph). This First Period house built by Deacon Peter Woodbury, the youngest son of "Old Planter" John Woodbury, remained the property of that family until 1902. Upon the death of Lucy S. Andrews, it was inherited by her daughter, Mabel Andrews Cressy, and her son, Arthur Cheever Cressy Jr. It is still in that family. The small structure at the corner of Frankwood Terrace was moved to the site during the Great Depression. It became famous locally for its caramel kisses and ice cream until around World War II, when it was removed and added to an ice-cream stand on Conant Street. (Courtesy Cressy Collection.)

"Would You Like a Kiss or an Ice Cream?" 82 Dodge Street (c. 1935 Photograph). Mr. and Mrs. William Trask appear to be holding up the sign that tempts motorists and pedestrians to try their nine delicious homemade ice-cream flavors. William Trask was the candy and ice cream maker, while his wife and their partners, the Leo Spinneys, served the public. (Courtesy Cressy Collection.)

A Basement Tree House, Corner of Dodge Street and Longwood Avenue (c. 1936 Photograph). Teenager Leslie H. Sigman fits perfectly into the asymmetrical trunk of the centuries-old tree before its removal from the site. (Courtesy Cressy Collection.)

Wenham Lake from the Beverly Shore (Early-20th-Century Postcard). One-third of the "Great Pond" is within the city limits of Beverly, which (along with Salem) uses the 320-acre site (34 feet above sea level) as a water supply. The Beverly Independent Ice Company, which was operated by the Clain family at 39 West Dane Street *c.* 1910, sold Wenham Lake Ice.

THE OPENING OF THE COMMODORE RESTAURANT, 45 ENON STREET (1955 PHOTOGRAPH). An eye-catching sign advertises the new eatery, which retained the nautical look of the former Robinson's Lighthouse Restaurant. Shown participating in the opening day ceremonies are, from left to right, John Frangos (who was born in Greece), Mayor Clarence Wilkinson, Mike Frangos, Spero Frangos, and Charlie Frangos. Many Boston area politicians attended the annual St. Patrick's Day dinner between 1970 and 1999, when the restaurant closed. (Courtesy Mike Frangos.)

THE LODGE POLE RANCH, BRIMBAL AVENUE (C. 1948 PHOTOGRAPH). Built *c.* 1900 and owned initially by attorney Otis Dunham, the multilevel entertainment spot was a popular retreat for Boston-area performers, such as Lionel and Diana Barrymore, John Carradine, Wallace Beery, Billy De Wolfe, and a host of starlets. Dunham supported the Native American people, collected their artifacts, and named the "ranch" for the decorative pole used in their ceremonies. A metal tepee on the grounds greeted guests. The building (roofed with terra-cotta tiles) fell into disrepair and was torn down in the late 1950s. (Courtesy David J. Dunham Sr.)

"MINE HOSTS" TED AND DORIS DUNHAM, THE LODGE POLE RANCH (C. 1948 PHOTOGRAPH). The Dunhams, who resided in the penthouse and who were the second and last owners of the ranch, pose with a Hollywood columnist (right) on one of the terraces. Every Saturday night during the season, Manuel's Black & White Orchestra performed in the Moorish Room for couples who paid the admission fee of $1.75. They could also have "special parties in the Mahogany Room," walk through the Tropical Garden, or use the bowling alleys. (Courtesy Dunham Collection.)

Eight

The North Shore Music Theatre

The First "Tent" of the North Shore Music Theatre, 62 Dunham Road (c. 1956 Photograph). Vintage 1950s automobiles park on the unpaved grounds of the city's first theatre in the round, which opened with great fanfare to the public during the 1954 summer season. Countless famous Broadway stage and Hollywood film stars (and other well-known entertainers) have made their way up and down the ramps that lead to the circular stage with the orchestra pit to one side. Whether taking a suite at the Hawthorne Hotel in Salem, or at the King's Grant Inn on Route 128 in nearby Danvers, the performers bring an air of excitement to the area when they are spotted locally. The present year-round, climate-controlled theatre was opened in 1989 with even greater fanfare than the first structure, with its fabric door flaps used by both actors and theatergoers. (Courtesy the North Shore Music Theatre.)

BETWEEN ACTS (1966 PHOTOGRAPH). Patrons and ticket holders rubberneck amidst artwork during a 12th season performance. Those who arrived early or had made reservations could have cocktails and dine at the Theatre Terrace Restaurant before the show, while those who preferred an after-theatre supper could dine then. At the buffet table, guests could select roast beef, Polynesian chicken, or seafood newburg (including a salad, rolls and butter, and coffee) for $2.95. They could enjoy a bottle of Cruse Rose for $3.15 or sparkling Mumm's Extra Dry champagne for $8.75. (Courtesy the North Shore Music Theatre.)

A FASHION SHOW AT THE MUSIC THEATRE (C. 1970 PHOTOGRAPH). Designed mainly for the female set, the fashion shows sponsored by the theatre proved to be a popular addition to the performances. Some tailgate antique shows were held on the grounds in the 1960s, much to the delight of antiques enthusiasts. (Courtesy the North Shore Music Theatre.)

AN EARLY MUSIC THEATRE POSTER (1963). One of the most famous film stars of the 20th century, Gloria Swanson, was 64 years old (slightly older than her disturbed character, Norma Desmond, in *Sunset Boulevard*) when she appeared in the new, short-lived comedy *Just for Tonight*. (Courtesy the North Shore Music Theatre.)

A MUSIC THEATRE DISPLAY IN FRONT OF THE BEVERLY NATIONAL BANK, 240 CABOT STREET (1969 PHOTOGRAPH). A young employee or friend of the theatre is in charge of the display that highlights the "Fabulous 15th Season," with stars such as Elaine Stritch, Jo Anne Worley, and Eddie Bracken scheduled to appear that summer. (Courtesy the North Shore Music Theatre.)

ANY WEDNESDAY (1968 PHOTOGRAPH). This drama starred Vivian Blaine, Dyan Cannon, Alan Yorke, and John Dutra as depicted in a minimalist setting. Plays by the likes of William Shakespeare and contemporary playwrights are salt-and-peppered throughout the theatre's season, but most audiences seem to prefer the tried and true big-name Broadway musicals with their familiar lyrics and melodies. (Courtesy the North Shore Music Theatre.)

"GLAD TO SIGN MY AUTOGRAPH" (1961 PHOTOGRAPH). The first star of the Broadway musical *Hello, Dolly!*, Carol Channing (b. 1923) pauses to flash her famous smile and sign a program for Augustus "Gus" Means, the former Republican state senator for the Third Essex District, who was then president of a car dealership. (Courtesy the North Shore Music Theatre.)

Nine

Beverly Cove

Hospital Point Light, off Neptune Street at the End of Bay View Avenue (Early-20th-Century Postcard). The white beacon shining from the 1871 lighthouse that alerts vessels along the shore also bathes the two bronze plaques with historical information on the nearby boulder. One plaque honors the valiant men of Beverly who manned the fort during the Revolutionary War. The other describes Hospital Point Light (which marks the deep water channel to Beverly, Salem, and Marblehead) and mentions the smallpox hospital that once stood on the hill at the rear. The Second Empire "cottage" built in the 1880s by the textile capitalist Amos A. Lawrence above the lighthouse was the first and most impressive one of its type encountered along the shore from the city proper. Beverly Cove begins at the corner of Hale and Lothrop Streets and wends its way to Pride's Crossing. Henry Cabot Lodge Jr. (1902–1985) was the most illustrious person to reside in "the Cove" during the 20th century. Lodge—who was a U.S. senator from Massachusetts, a 1960 vice presidential nominee of the Republican party, and a distinguished diplomat—lived with his wife, Emily, and children, George and Harry, at 275 Hale Street.

RECEIVING THE COLLEGE CHARTER (1939 PHOTOGRAPH). Gov. Leverett Saltonstall (left) presents the official document incorporating Endicott Junior College to its president, the Reverend George O. Bierkoe, while his wife, Dean Eleanor Tupper, beams with pleasure. Established as a two-year "career junior college for young women," and now a four-year coeducational institution known as Endicott College, its buildings and campus occupy more than 200 acres of breathtaking shorefront and wooded property. (Courtesy Endicott College.)

COLLEGE HALL, ENDICOTT COLLEGE, 376 HALE STREET (C. 1945 PHOTOGRAPH). Dressed for fall, these students are leaving the stone building that was constructed *c.* 1917 by Isabella Stuart Gardner of Boston fame for her nephew, William Amory Gardner. Acquired in 1939, the building was first used for "career education classes," including course titles such as Art, Clothing, Home Management, Merchandising, Secretarial Science, and Tearoom Management. It is now the administration building. (Courtesy Endicott College.)

REYNOLDS HALL, ENDICOTT COLLEGE, 376 HALE STREET (C. 1955 PHOTOGRAPH). For many years, this Queen Anne–style house had been the Kendall School for Girls. It was the first property purchased in 1939 by the college and renamed to honor Dr. Grace Morrison Reynolds, an original trustee and former president of the General Federation of Woman's Clubs. The four original founders of Endicott College were Clarence Tupper; his wife, Ella Webster Tupper; their daughter, Eleanor Tupper; and her husband, George O. Bierkoe. (Courtesy Endicott College.)

A GRADUATION REHEARSAL IN FRONT OF TUPPER HALL, ENDICOTT COLLEGE, 376 HALE STREET (C. 1952 PHOTOGRAPH). Named for John Endecott, who became governor of the Massachusetts Bay Colony in 1649, the junior college was approved by the Commonwealth of Massachusetts to grant Associate in Arts and Associate in Science degrees beginning in 1944. Three years earlier, in 1941, the first class graduated with 19 students. In 1952, it was accredited by the New England Association of Schools and Colleges. Behind the students is the former summer home of the Bryce Allen family, owners of the Moore-McCormick Steamship Lines. The waterfront property was acquired by the college in 1942–1943 and was named to honor Clarence Tupper. (Courtesy Endicott College.)

MINGO BEACH HILL, HALE STREET (EARLY-20TH-CENTURY POSTCARD). Endicott College students enjoy the ocean view from this vantage point as they walk between classes or power-walk for exercise.

MINGO BEACH, OFF HALE STREET (1905 POSTCARD). This small, crescent-shaped beach was supposedly named for Robin Mingo, a black slave owned by Thomas Woodbury. He was one of the 28 slaves owned by town inhabitants in 1754. Mingo's master promised him freedom "when the tide should recede so far as to leave a dry passage between the shore and 'Becky's Hedge.'" This only happened once—the year Mingo died in 1773.

Ten

PRIDE'S CROSSING

THE PRIDE'S CROSSING RAILROAD STATION, HALE STREET OPPOSITE PAINE AVENUE (C. 1907 POSTCARD). The area called Pride's Crossing along Beverly's Gold Coast is somewhat vague, and property lines overlap on turn-of-the-century atlases. However, officials at the local post office state that Pride's, as it is commonly called, is between 407 and 600 Hale Street. The locale's name is associated with early resident, John Pride, who was granted land in 1636. His descendant, Peter Pride, built an early-18th-century dwelling on the site at 584 Hale Street. Some summer residents of note included in the 1893 *Blue Book of Beverly* are Col. and Mrs. Jerome Bonaparte; Martin Brimmer, a noted Boston businessman and early patron of the Museum of Fine Arts, Boston; and Mrs. Nicholas Roosevelt Longworth, the daughter of Teddy Roosevelt. In the mid-20th century, Count and Countess Francisco M. Guardabassi resided at the "Old Fort" on exclusive Paine Avenue. The 1879 Queen Anne–style mansion was designed by the prestigious architectural firm of McKim, Mead and Bigelow. It was built for Francis Lee Higginson near the remains of an early fort.

THE LANDMARK SCHOOL, 412 HALE STREET. Formerly the residence of Mr. and Mrs. Bayard Warren, and sited on a hill overlooking the Atlantic Ocean, the property was acquired in 1971 by the Landmark School, the students of which learn to overcome language-based learning disabilities. Now known as Norrie House to honor Edith Norrie, the founder of the movement to help dyslexics in Denmark, the 35-room Georgian–style brick structure serves multiple purposes. (Courtesy Landmark School.)

THE AMES AND COTTING BEACH, OFF HALE STREET (EARLY-20TH-CENTURY POSTCARD). The imposing Oliver Ames and Charles U. Cotting estates shared a long pier for easy access to their yachts and for the convenience of visitors. (Courtesy Beverly Public Library.)

On the Beverly Coast, Massachusetts (1874 Engraving after the Oil Painting by John F. Kensett, 1816–1872). Two men sit in a clearing near a rocky cliff surrounded by weather-beaten trees somewhere along the 7-mile stretch of the shoreline. The American poet and editor James Russell Lowell wrote in 1854 that in Beverly "the country and sea-shore are combined . . . in the most charming way."

The Cochrane-Sears House, Paine Avenue. America's first tennis champion, Richard D. Sears, resided in this Shingle-style dwelling, which was built *c.* 1880 a mere stone's, or tennis ball's throw from the churning ocean. Interior spaces include a grand front hall with wide staircase and a large, carved limestone fireplace surround; a living room with raised deal (wood) carving from a castle in Bristol, England; and an oval dining room with built-in sideboards and numerous windows overlooking the estate. (Courtesy John W. Sears.)

Hale Street Looking toward Thissell Street (c. 1935 Postcard). Many sections of the distinctive $100,000 wrought-iron fence on the right side of the street, where the former Frick family stable is located, were patriotically removed by Helen Frick during World War II and were donated as scrap iron for the cause. (Courtesy Beverly Public Library.)

The Entrance Gates to Eagle Rock, 453 Hale Street. Stately square limestone columns with a quartet of carved neoclassical urns and a pair of eagles grace the entrance gates to the most lavish estate ever erected on the North Shore. Obvious ostentatious splendor as displayed by the summer residents provoked the city's first mayor, the Honorable John I. Baker, to take steps to thwart what he determined was tax evasion. (Courtesy Thomas L. Creamer.)

EAGLE ROCK, FORMERLY LOCATED AT 453 HALE STREET (EARLY-20TH-CENTURY POSTCARD). Henry Clay Frick—the merciless multimillionaire steel magnate who became chairman of Carnegie Steel in Pittsburgh, Pennsylvania—spared no expense to build this mansion, dubbed in its day the "Versailles of the Gold Coast." Architect Arthur Little also designed neighboring mansions for Edwin C. Swift (Swiftmoore), and for William H. Moore (Rockmarge). Guests were thrilled to be invited to a soirée at Eagle Rock, but many were not so thrilled with Frick himself. To ameliorate some of the animosity directed at him, in 1908 the Pride's Crossing potentate presented the high school with scientific apparatus. The Frick family always traveled in style, arriving at the local train station in their private luxury railroad car.

THE ENTRANCE TO PAINE AVENUE, OFF HALE STREET (C. 1900 POSTCARD). One of the oldest such avenues on the North Shore and one with the most "summer homes," Paine Avenue is situated opposite the Pride's Crossing railroad station. A turn-of-the-century observer noted that avenues in the area "are covered with fine crushed rock and are as smooth as a pool table. They are raked every day and new crushed rock is sprinkled upon them every few weeks." (Courtesy Beverly Public Library.)

THE RESIDENCE OF WILLIAM S. AND JOHN T. SPAULDING, PAINE AVENUE (EARLY-20TH-CENTURY POSTCARD). Large flower-filled urns, lush vegetation, and striped awnings impart a look of grandeur to Sunset Rock, the home shared by the Spauldings. Located on the extensive property was a classical garden with marble statuary behind a stepped, moatlike arrangement and an arched wooden chinoiserie bridge nearby.

A Partial View of Avalon (c. 1915 Postcard). Only visible from the ocean, the summer residence built in 1907 by textile manufacturer Frederick Ayer of Lowell was situated until recently on one of the roads at the end of Paine Avenue. An August 1922 article in the *Beverly Evening Times* touted Avalon as being an "ideal home" for Pres. Warren G. Harding "if he makes his much heralded cruise along the Maine coast in the *Mayflower* and tarries for awhile in the Garden City of the North Shore."

The Front Entrance of Avalon, Paine Avenue (c. 1915 Photograph). Avalon was designed by the landscape and architectural firm of J. Olmsted of Boston. The Beverly Farms contracting firm of Connolly Brothers built the solid, stucco-faced structure. In addition to the incredible view, meticulously landscaped grounds, and privacy, Mr. Ayer's summer residence was a three-story showplace with five chambers and several guest bathrooms. A later owner renovated the mansion by removing the three sections of red tile roof and the dominant triangular pediment with dentils, creating a flat roofline. Fortunately, the structure was meticulously documented and all the architectural elements were removed before it was demolished. (Courtesy George W. Newman III.)

AVALON'S LIVING ROOM (C. 1915 PHOTOGRAPH). The Ayer family living room, or parlor, featured chinoiserie wallpaper that shimmered with the glow of reflected light from the electrified ormolu sconces. Swagged satin jabots and plush velvet upholstery added to the décor of the room, where the family undoubtedly entertained neighbors such as Mrs. Loring at Burnside, Mrs. Henry Clay Frick at Eagle Rock, and the Kings and Spauldings at "stone-tunneled Sunset Rock." (Courtesy Newman Collection.)

AVALON'S ENTRANCE HALL (C. 1915 PHOTOGRAPH). Probably the most impressive interior architectural feature of the Ayer estate was the welcoming elliptical entrance hall, which on sunny days was filled with bright light. (Courtesy Newman Collection.)

ROCKMARGE, PAINE AVENUE (EARLY-20TH-CENTURY POSTCARD). The palatial mansion built by William Henry Moore in 1905 featured eight large fluted columns and a full-length piazza. Nicknamed "Judge," the Utica, New York capitalist owned the National Biscuit Company and the Diamond Match Company. He was involved in the control of monopolies, the watering of stocks, and was the owner of a railroad as well. An expert horse handler, Moore drove his spit-and-polish carriages around the area with great flair. (Courtesy Clayton Collection.)

THE CARRIAGE HOUSE AT ROCKMARGE, PAINE AVENUE. One large and two smaller domes are featured on the immense carriage house that still inspires awe and gives an idea of the former mansion's size. W.H. Moore's pampered 38 thoroughbred horses certainly lived in style! (Courtesy private collection.)

SWIFTMOORE, PAINE AVENUE (EARLY-20TH-CENTURY POSTCARD). Mourners were brought by a special train to this estate to pay their respects to Edward Carleton Swift, who died there a few years after the completion of the mansion. The owner of the largest beef-packing firm in the country, he maintained a stock and poultry farm at 219 Brimbal Avenue, which was then managed by his widow, Florence A. Swift

ELEONORA SEARS (EARLY-20TH-CENTURY PHOTOGRAPH). The daughter of socialites F.R. Sears Jr. and the former Eleonora Randolph Coolidge, "Eleo" Sears (1881–1968) was a financially independent and outspoken athlete who excelled in such male-dominated sports as polo (when in 1909 she shocked Burlingame, Californians by wearing men's apparel at a match), squash, swimming, and tennis. A long-distance walker, Eleo flew planes, drove racecars, and was involved in horse show activities, steeple chasing, and flat racing. She had a lifelong love of the theater. (Courtesy Sears Collection.)

Eleven

BEVERLY FARMS

BEVERLY FARMS SQUARE (EARLY-20TH-CENTURY POSTCARD). The well-known "Farms" is in the eastern part of the city. Its small-town commercial center begins at the corner of Hale and West Streets in front of the fire station. Some Beverly Farms summer residents of note listed in the 1893 *Blue Book of Beverly* include Dr. and Mrs. Oliver Wendell Holmes and their son, Judge Oliver Wendell Holmes; Col. Henry Lee of Boston; and members of the Cabot, Cochrane, Richardson, Shattuck, and Weld families. Lucy Larcom, the author and poet who wrote *Wild Roses of Cape Ann* (1880), enjoyed living at the Farms during that period of her life and career.

THE WILLIAM HASKELL HOUSE, 680 HALE STREET (EARLY-20TH-CENTURY POSTCARD). Around the time this photograph was taken, the lean-to house was the property of F. Gordon Dexter, but had remained in the same family of Haskells for about six generations since it was built in 1689. Sited at an angle to the street, the house is somewhat between the Shingle-style St. Margaret's Church at the crest of the hill on the same side of Hale Street and St. John's Episcopal church on the opposite side of the main street that leads into Beverly Farms.

ST. JOHN'S EPISCOPAL CHURCH, 701 HALE STREET (C. 1940S POSTCARD). "The scene of brilliant society weddings," the Tudor-style, stone church was built shortly after the congregation was organized on June 17, 1900. Interestingly, the Beverly city directory for 1915 states that "all seats [are] free." (Courtesy Clayton Collection.)

A View along West Street (c. 1915 Postcard). The railroad crossing sign in the distance is identified with the nearby station and is where the commercial section of the Farms ends. Adjacent to Neighbor's Hall, with its stone arches, is the fire station where on October 15, 1944, Beverly officials and dignitaries gathered to dedicate the town's honor roll of World War II soldiers and sailors. The first floor of Marshall's Hall on the corner of Hale and West Street was where F.W. Varney, the registered apothecary had his store for many years. As well as carrying daily and Sunday newspapers, Varney made "a specialty of compounding physicians' prescriptions. This department is fully stocked with reliable and up-to-date remedies and is constantly under the supervision of Graduates of the Pharmacy [in Boston] of long experience." (Courtesy Thomas Collection.)

The Beverly Farms Train Station, Oak Street opposite Vine Street (Early-20th-Century Postcard). A fancifully shaped, wide overhanging roof protected Victorian-period passengers from the elements, while later commuters and travelers had more room, but less ambiance, under this elongated roof.

THE WEST BEACH PIER, OFF HALE STREET (C. 1900 POSTCARD). Incorporated on April 28, 1852, by local residents, West Beach is still private. The signs near the entrance and the one in this image state that "this pier [is] for the sole use of the members of the West Beach Corporation and Subscribers." The exclusive beach is part of the original grant of land made to John Blackleach, who later transferred it to John West. At one time, Thomas West had a landing place near the corporation's bathhouse.

A HOME TO TWO HOLMES, 868 HALE STREET (EARLY-20TH-CENTURY POSTCARD). In 1908, Dr. Oliver Wendell Holmes (1809–1894), the author of *The Autocrat of the Breakfast-Table,* purchased the Marshall estate and summered here with his family. His son, Oliver Wendell Holmes Jr. (1841–1935), vacationed here as well. The younger Holmes, a respected jurist, was an associate justice of the U.S. Supreme Court between 1902 and 1932. (Courtesy Beverly Public Library.)

Twelve

MISCELLANEOUS BEVERLYANA

THE CENTERVILLE IMPROVEMENT SOCIETY (C. 1935 PHOTOGRAPH). Members of the Centerville Improvement Society wear old-fashioned costumes and gather around the vintage stagecoach to document a parade they have participated in. The three prominent buildings in this section of Beverly include the Centerville Church at 135 Standley Street, the Centerville Improvement Society at 437 Essex Street, and the adjacent former Engine House, No. 4. (Courtesy Judy Terry.)

THE NORTH BAR, BEVERLEY, ENGLAND (EARLY-20TH-CENTURY PHOTOGRAPH). The English market town known as Beverley Minster has been suggested as one prototype name for the Garden City. Possibly dating to the second century, Beverley is the capital of the East Riding of Yorkshire and is 182 miles north of London. Boasting an impressive Gothic cathedral, it was the 11th largest town in medieval England. (Schier Collection.)

A SHIPBOARD GATHERING (1907 PHOTOGRAPH). The Joseph F. Clayton family, who resided at 28 Atlantic Avenue, embarked on a European vacation with the express purpose to visit Beverley, England. City patrolman Joseph (second from the left), his wife, Hattie (probably behind him), their son, George, two other unidentified couples (possibly Beverlyites), and two employees of the *Saxonia* (one being very camera shy), pose for this impromptu picture, which was made into a postcard and sent to their relatives and friends back home. (Courtesy Clayton Collection.)

The First Baptist Baseball Club (Early-20th-Century Photograph). Teenage members of the club, which was associated with the Foss Bible Class, line up wearing their new uniforms stitched with a Gothic letter *B*. Standing second from left in the front is Earl Wardell, who died shortly after this picture was taken. His bereft fellow team members kept his memory alive in all their games. The other players include, from left to right, the following: (front row) Andy Hammond, Brian Newton, Allan Foss, and Paul Nelson; (back row) Frank Nelson, two Douglas brothers, and Master Browne. (Courtesy First Baptist Church of Beverly.)

Howard Johnson's Restaurant, Route 128 at Exit 9 (c. 1949 Postcard). Grilled hot dogs or hamburgers (followed by the difficult decision of what 28-flavor ice cream to choose) made a visit to "Ho-Jo's" a memorable treat. Everyone was familiar with the chain of turnpike restaurants with the bright red roof begun by Howard Johnson of Quincy, Massachusetts, around the early 1940s.

A "Harvest Time" Gathering, Centerville Christian Endeavor Church, 135 Standley Street (c. 1940s Photograph). Doted upon by adoring mothers, these somewhat patriotically dressed children pose for a local early fall parade to celebrate the end of summer and the beginning of a new season. (Courtesy Judy Kent.)

A Promotional Prize Presented at the Atlantic Motor Mart Inc., 443–445 Rantoul Street (1954 Photograph). Robert H. Gove's winning essay on how much he enjoyed his new automobile netted him an equally new Westinghouse portable black and white television set with stylish bent rod feet. His essay is held, and the television is being presented by either Daniel F. Pierre, the president and treasurer of the firm, or Frank Pierre, the vice president. (Courtesy Gove Collection.)

THE BEVERLY SUNOCO SERVICE STATION, 78 CABOT STREET (C. 1950S PHOTOGRAPH). Bold and colorful plastic decorative motifs used on commercial buildings, such as this caduceus on the gas station at the corner of Pleasant Street, are now icons of nostalgia. Hiram M. Dexter was the proprietor of the service station, which charged slightly over 23¢ per gallon for custom blended gasoline at this time. (Courtesy Larcom Collection.)

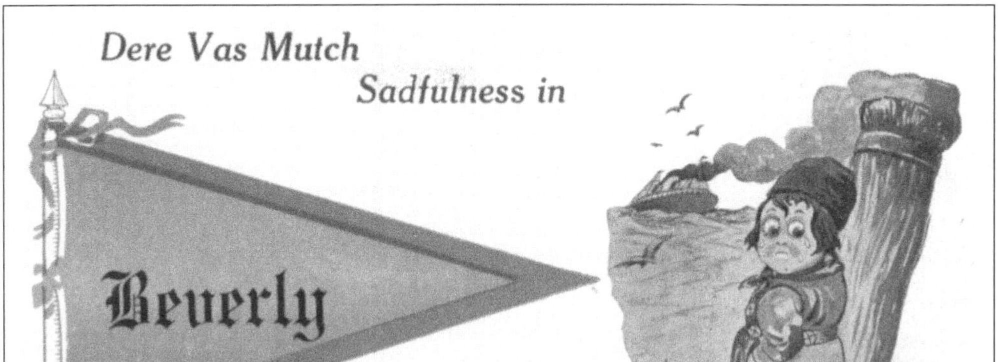

A GENERIC GREETING (EARLY-20TH-CENTURY POSTCARD). Even a flower-loving Dutch boy with patched pants and wooden shoes can shed a tear when a friend leaves Beverly for a distant shore, until the special person returns once again to the Garden City.

Acknowledgments

The author is indebted to the following individuals, many of whom have shared their images, as well as their knowledge of Beverly's history. Included in the running list are the following: Mr. and Mrs. Robert W. Atherton, Will Barnet, Mr. and Mrs. Kenneth H. Clayton, Arthur Cheever Cressy Jr., David J. Dunham Sr., Mr. and Mrs. Dan Durrell, William Finch and Carol Rose, Mike Frangos, Judy Kent, Mr. and Mrs. Edward L. Kransberg, Paul S. Larcom, Alvin Mitchell, Mr. and Mrs. Ralph A. Parisella, Erik A.R. Ronnberg Jr., Stephen J. Schier, John W. Sears, Rita St. Pierre, Judy Terry, Gary Thomas, Ruth Robb Wolcott, and Mr. and Mrs. Paul Zaido.

Also thanked for their assistance are these business owners or employees of institutions: Webster Bull, Commonwealth Editions; William Cummings, Barry McDonough, and Jim Trudeau, Cummings Properties; Robert W. Gove, Gove Lumber Company; Charles Harris, Deedee Grace, and Jana Pokrief, Landmark School; Russell Kiernan, Marine Art Gallery; Brenda Koskinen and Joanne Glick, Appleseeds; James K. Polese and Barbara Dempsey, North Shore Music Theatre; F. Elliott and Dave Rowand, Rowand's; Ellen Sheehan, Cabot Street Cinema Theatre; Patricia Small, First Baptist Church of Beverly; and Henry Swanson and John J.Keohane, Henry's of North Beverly.

For their expertise in diagnosing and remedying a malfunctioning computer during the 11th hour, the author praises Thomas L. Creamer and his youthful associate, Tim Kwiatek.

And for editing the manuscript for historical facts, Barbara F. Broudo, director of archives-museum, Endicott College; and Thomas F. Scully, director of the Beverly Public Library, are similarly thanked.

Bibliography

Barber, John Warner. *Historical Collections of Every Town in Massachusetts*. Worcester, Mass.: Dorr, Howland & Company, 1839.

Bentley, William, D.D. *The Diary of William Bentley, D.D.* Gloucester, Mass.: Peter Smith, 1962.

Garland, Joseph E. *The North Shore*. Beverly, Mass.: Commonwealth Editions, 1998.

Hoisington, Daniel J. *Made in Beverly: A History of Beverly Industry*. Beverly, Mass.: Beverly Historic District Commission, 1989.

Hurd, D. Hamilton. *History of Essex County, Massachusetts*. Philadelphia, Pa.: J.W. Lewis & Co., 1888.

Goss, K. David, and Ronald N. Tagney. *Treasures of a Seaport Town*. Beverly, Mass.: The Beverly Historical Society and Museum, 1998.

Parnell, Howard, ed. *100 Years of the Beverly Times: Then & Now*. Beverly, Mass.: Essex County Newspapers, 1993.

Shepley, Hayden. *Automobiles Built in Essex County, Massachusetts*. Toughkenamon, Pa.: Hayden Shepley, 1976.

Stone, Edwin M. *History of Beverly*. Boston, Mass.: James Munroe and Company, 1843.

Symmes, Richard W. *North Beverly Remembered*. Concord, N.H.: The Village Press, Inc., 1982. Beverly History File, Beverly Public Library.